The Makings of a Doctor

By

James Griffin

ISBN No: 978-1-903172-76-6

Publishers: Barny Books
                Hough on the Hill,
                Grantham,
                Lincolnshire
                NG32 2BB

                Tel: 01400 250246
                www.barnybooks.biz

Dedicated to my wife, Catherine

in thanks for her unfailing support

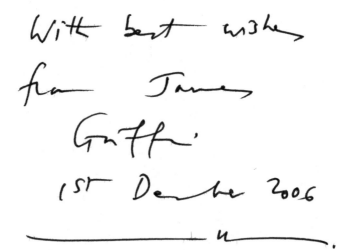

With best wishes
from James
Griffin
1st December 2006

Contents

Angry Albert

The phone rang at 6 am. An old man's voice roared, "Is that you Roberts? Get yourself out here and examine our Maggie. She's in a bad way."

"I'm sorry," I stammered, as I awoke from a deep sleep. "Who's calling?"

"Who do you think's calling?" came the angry reply. "And who are you anyway?"

Before I could gather my thoughts, the voice continued, "Where's that two armed robber Roberts?"

"Dr Roberts is not available." I said, trying to keep my voice calm.

"Not available … what do you mean, not available?"

"Dr Roberts is on holiday. I'm Dr Griffin. I'm covering for him." The man's rudeness had caught me completely unawares.

There was a second's silence followed by a snort of disapproval.

"Well Griffin, you listen to me then. I want you out here right now to sort out our Maggie."

"What's wrong with Maggie?" I asked trying to get some idea of what he was talking about.

"How would I know what's wrong with her? Why do you think I phoned? I'm not a big earning Doc like you, am I? That's your job to know what's wrong with her." He was obviously pleased with himself at putting me in my place.

His reply was guaranteed to needle most doctors – especially at six o'clock in the morning.

I didn't speak for a second or two as I took a deep breath.

"Have you gone back to sleep, Griffin, or is there something the matter with you?" the voice sneered.

"Could I have your name and address please?" I asked, as politely as I could.

"Albert's me name," he answered sullenly.

"Albert who?"

"Everybody in Slievegart knows Albert,"

"I bet they do," I thought as I said, "I'm sorry, I'm not from Slievegart, I've only just arrived here and I don't know any Albert's. Could you please give me your full name and address and directions to your house."

As a medical student I was taught to be polite to patients, no matter how rude they were. Albert was pushing that teaching to the limits.

The phone remained silent for a long time. I began to wonder if Albert was going to speak again. The strain of dealing with him had my heart racing. A trickle of perspiration rolled down my brow. Albert obviously considered he had been given a ticking off and didn't seem to like it one little bit.

"Could you please give me ..." I began to say again.

"I heard you the first time sonny boy," Albert's cross voice interrupted. "I'll tell you where I live and I'll tell you once so you'd better listen."

He rattled out directions and ended up saying in a surly tone, "Now Griffin, you get yourself out here right this minute or you'll be hearing from my lawyer if anything happens to Maggie. She's bleeding to death."

He slammed down the phone before I could say another word. I leapt out of bed in a panic. This was my first night on call as a General Practitioner and Albert's was the fourth call that night.

I had been out to three patients at different ends of the Practice. I was feeling totally shattered and now I was faced with a woman bleeding to death in the middle of nowhere and her hostile husband threatening to sue me before I even got there.

"I'm too young for this sort of grief," I thought as I pulled on my shoes. I grabbed my jacket and ran downstairs and pulled open the solid oak front door.

I came out into a glorious summer's morning. Despite my anxiety I caught my breath at the beauty that greeted me. For several seconds my spirits lifted as I gazed across the luxurious lawns and hedges of Dr Robert's home and down through the small fields with their stone walls and white cottages to the sea glistening in the distance like a silver pond.

The rugged hills of the Kerry mountains rose spectacularly behind me, casting their shadows along the purple heather that tumbled down the grassy slopes. Everything was bathed in sunlight as birds chattered in the early morning and hopped through the blossoming flowers and bushes. A cuckoo called from the safety of a tall tree. I spotted Dr Roberts' golden retriever stretching herself lazily under the shade of a pine tree and then settle back to sleep after a prolonged yawn.

"I wish I had your life," I thought ruefully as I raced towards Dr Roberts rickety Landrover.

I never wanted to be a doctor and if this, my first day practising on my own, was typical of a doctors life, I wished I'd become a teacher, a plumber, a monk, anything other than a doctor.

My father was a doctor. My mother was a doctor. Two of my brothers and two of my sisters were doctors. The family was full of doctors.

From as early as I can remember I wanted to be an airline pilot and wear a smart uniform and a cap with gold braid. I wanted to fly Boeing 707s all over the world. My father didn't think much of my flying aspirations. He didn't say anything but hoped I'd grow out of it. He would have liked me to become a doctor like him and join him in his country practice and eventually take it over.

I had seen what his life was like as a village G.P. and it didn't appeal to me at all, especially the business of getting up in the middle of the night and being on call at all hours. I wanted a much more glamorous life altogether.

My ambitions took a nose dive when I looked into flying more seriously and checked on the academic qualifications needed to be a pilot. I was better at languages than science and thought with all that foreign travel they would be top of the list. They weren't even mentioned. Physics seemed to be essential and if there was one subject I couldn't understand, it was physics. No matter how hard I tried, it remained a perfect blank. As far as physics was concerned, I was dyslexic.

I didn't know what to do when fate took a hand.

At a school medical examination, the doctor told me I was short sighted and needed glasses. Any ambition I had of ever flying a Boeing 707 had just run into a brick wall.

'A' levels were looming and I was suddenly landed in a position where I had to come up with a new career plan – and quickly. It wasn't easy. I had spent years dreaming about becoming a pilot and never considered anything else.

My father was delighted my intention of flying had crash landed. He pretended he was sorry but I knew he was really pleased. He urged me to do medicine.

"Maybe you should consider medicine, James," he said. "You'd be surprised how interesting it is. I always thought you were cut out to be a doctor anyway, although you would have made a good pilot too," he added diplomatically. "But you'll make an even better doctor." He was never above using a bit a flattery to get what he wanted.

"If you find you don't like medicine," he added, "you can always change your mind and do something else. One thing about a medical degree is it opens the door to a lot of different types of work."

He went on to list people who had qualified as doctors and followed completely different careers.

"Look at Somerset Maughan and John Keats, the great English poet and Arthur Conan Doyle and Chekov. They were all doctors before becoming famous writers," he said enthusiastically.

"That lot bore me to tears especially Chekov" I said with little interest, "he makes me depressed."

My father would have to come up with something better.

"Well then," he said, not the least bit daunted. "What about Che Guevara and James Joyce. Young people seem to admire them for some reason. They were both medical students."

"Would you want me to end up like either of them – one writing gibberish at the end of his days and the other getting himself shot?"

"Well no, I don't suppose I would. I hadn't that in mind, I thought you might have admired them."

"I admire them as much as I admire a pig in muck," I retorted. I was still annoyed at not being able to be a pilot.

"Right, well then. That's them off the list. I can see they're not your type of hero." My father was beginning to sound a little bit less sure of himself.

He thought for a few seconds before trying again.

"Right then James. What about that half wit who has been on the TV recently. You seem to think he's very funny, though he's not in the slightest. It's that silly programme with a silly name – called after a snake at the circus or something like that. Anyway, I heard he was a doctor."

"Do you mean Monty Python's Flying Circus?" I said with sudden interest.

"Yes, that's it. That's the daft name. One of those fools is a doctor, Graham somebody or other."

"You mean Graham Chapman?" I loved Monty Python humour.

"Yes that's the boyo. He studied medicine at Cambridge apparently, if you could believe half of what you hear."

"How do you know that?"

"A patient in the surgery said recently you get doctors nowadays doing the oddest of jobs and mentioned him."

"So Graham Chapman's a doctor," I thought. "He can be hilariously funny, especially when he's not smutty. Maybe there could be something in this doctoring business after all."

My father's arguments finally persuaded me. I applied to medical Colleges in Ireland and England although I didn't think I had much chance of being accepted. My A level results were not expected to be spectacular.

To my surprise, Trinity College, Dublin offered me a place in their medical faculty provided I achieved three A level subjects at Grade D.

I couldn't believe it. It was too good to be true. Three A levels at Grade D. Even I could manage that. Today Medical Colleges require at least 3 As at A level. Fortunately for me, that wasn't the case in the late 1960s.

I got the grades and spent several happy, hectic years as a medical student in Dublin. I passed my final medical examinations in the early 1970s with a feeling of relief that I could put all that study behind me but also with a sense of loss at leaving behind so many friends and such a vibrant city.

I was undecided what to do as I approached the end of my houseman's year. I didn't know whether I wanted to do hospital medicine or become a G.P. when my consultant asked me at the end of my last ward round with him if I would be interested in doing a four month locum for a friend of his – a Dr Roberts – who was a G.P. in a quiet fishing village in County Kerry.

The way the Consultant described the practice, it sounded idyllic. My next post didn't start until the end of October – four months later - so that suited me fine.

I phoned Dr Roberts that evening. He sounded pleasant though a little eccentric.

"Can you drive a landrover, James?" was his first question. When I assured him I could, he said, "Well then, you're the right man for this Practice. I'll see you tomorrow." He suggested a generous payment and arranged to meet me at the station the following morning.

Early the next morning, I took the train down to Tralee, Dr Roberts met me standing beside his beautiful sleek silver Jaguar. He was, as his voice suggested, a colourful character – jovial, portly and dressed in a three-piece suit with a burgundy bow tie. He welcomed me so effusively, I thought he was going to hug me. He thanked me for coming down to Slievegart so promptly.

"It's a ton weight off my mind James, you arriving here so soon."

The journey back to Slievegart passed quickly as he regaled me with stories about his life spent in General Practice in the village. We drove up from the coast to his home on a hill overlooking the sea. Dr Roberts introduced me to his equally charming wife, Stella, before giving me a quick tour of his old world house.

It was huge. Ivy crept up the outside walls almost to the roof. Bay windows gave commanding views of the sea. There were two sitting rooms and a dining room with solid oak doors, chandeliers and enormous carved fireplaces. Deep comfortable furniture was tastefully placed around the main sitting room. With its wood panelled walls and high ceilings, it would have been the perfect place to curl up with a book beside a turf fire on a winter's evening or to throw open the bay windows and let the sea breeze sweep through on a summer's day.

A surgery and waiting room was attached to one side of the house. Dr Roberts showed me his consulting room with its large roll top desk and swivelling Captain's chair. Colourful paintings covered the yellow ochre walls. There was a faint smell of carbolic soap and ether.

The doctor seemed to be in a hurry as he pointed out instruments he thought I would need. As soon as he finished talking about one, he launched on to the next one. I found myself being rushed from room to room as if we were in the Derby. His tongue kept pace with his movement. There was no pause in his flow to give me a chance to ask a question.

I noticed that most of the equipment looked prehistoric. His stethoscope, with its thick rubber tubing and heavy metal head looked like it had been built in a shipyard. I don't think his blood pressure apparatus, in its thick mahogany box, had been recalibrated since he bought it thirty five years before. There were wicked looking instruments for extracting teeth, suturing lacerations and removing bladder stones.

He sterilized the instruments he used by boiling them in a battered saucepan he kept specifically for that purpose on the Aga cooker in the kitchen which was next door to his surgery.

As we moved quickly back into the house, he pointed out with pride, a shelf of green and brown medical bottles with exotic Latin labels and ground glass stoppers but didn't have time to tell me what they were for.

Dr Roberts continued to talk rapidly about his practice as he and Stella marched out the front door and down the steps to their Jaguar. They only paused to pat the head of Bonnie the dog and stroke the two cats and whisper a few words into their ears. Dr Roberts was still talking as he climbed into his car and started coasting down the drive, leaving me standing on the steps with my mouth open, trying to get a question in.

"I hope you don't mind looking after Bonnie and the two cats while we're away. They're great friends and they all sleep in the same kennel and eat the same food. They shouldn't be too much trouble." He finished by saying that was all he had time for as they were leaving immediately to catch the evening ferry from Rosslare to France. I'd expected at least a couple of days to get into the swing of things.

His parting words to me as he lit his pipe in a cloud of aromatic smoke was, "Now, James, if you have any problems, give my colleague Dr Sylvester O'Flathertie a call. He's the only other doctor in the village. You might find him a bit unusual but he is a top class clinician," Then, with a hoot on the horn and smiles on their faces, they were off and I had the house, the practice, two cats and a dog and a couple of thousand patients to myself.

I wondered afterwards what Dr Roberts would have done if I had told him I couldn't do his four month locum. How would he have got off to France in time for his grand tour? He was obviously one of those men who make their own luck.

Those thoughts were at the back of my mind as I made my way to Albert's home and his Maggie, praying I would be in time.

Bleeding can be very serious. It depends on the site and severity of the bleeding as well as numerous other factors. Quite a lot of elderly patients are on Warfarin (rat poison) to thin their blood and stop clots forming in their veins or heart. If these people cut themselves, they bleed for much longer than normal. I was once called to see an old man on Warfarin who couldn't get the bleeding on his chin to stop after he nicked himself shaving.

A laceration to the jugular vein or carotid artery can cause death within minutes whereas even a deep cut to the arm or leg, unless it hits an artery, is not immediately life threatening.

I thought anxiously about those conditions as I clambered into the Landrover and headed up into the foothills of the Kerry mountains. Even with my anxiety I was able, momentarily, to appreciate the extraordinary beauty of the early morning sun rising over the Kerry hilltops.

"How am I ever going to find out where that ignoramus, Albert, lives?" I thought as I turned into the narrow mountainous roads, "and will his wife have bled to death by the time I get there?"

After twenty minutes of frenetic driving along tiny bumpy lanes edged on either side by low stone walls that sometimes were all that stood between me and a precipitous fall into the Atlantic, I somehow stumbled on Albert's run down cottage.

It was at the edge of a remote country lane. The lane was overgrown with brambles and ferns that almost met in the middle. How did Albert and Maggie make their way through it without tearing themselves to pieces, I wondered? The Landrover bumped in and out of potholes that were like small craters as I raced towards the house

The front door was open. I jumped out of the Landrover and charged through it nearly knocking down an old grey woman who was sweeping the hallway. She moved aside silently without looking up.

An elderly man stood at the hallway window peering through an old telescope as if expecting to see an invading army gallop up out of the valley. He didn't look up either as I raced into the living room.

I had no trouble recognizing Albert. He sat sprawled on a reinforced armchair with his back to the door. He was reading a newspaper which he had selected from an untidy pile of old papers that lay beside his chair.

In front of him lay the collapsed form of Maggie. She looked pale and lifeless and was surrounded by a pool of dark blood which stretched out almost to Albert's enormous slippered feet.

I was dumbfounded by the sight of a man reading a paper so calmly as his wife lay bleeding to death at his feet.

I moved through the clutter of the room to stand in front of him. I stared in amazement at the lifeless Maggie.

"How long has she been lying here?" I gasped.

Albert put his newspaper down with an irritated snort, to reveal a huge, red face that had been cross for a lifetime.

"How would I know?" he snapped as he looked me up and down disapprovingly. "She was here when I came down this morning."

I decided not to get involved in a futile argument.

"Could you please phone for an ambulance while I see to Maggie?" I said as I hastily opened my medical bag.

Albert gave me an angry look and, flicking his paper up, began to read again. He seemed totally unconcerned about the critical condition of his wife.

I was staggered by his indifference as I leant over Maggie and checked the pulse in her neck. It was there but only just. I was alarmed. I never had to deal with anything like this before in my short medical career and in such a setting. At my teaching hospital, if I was called to a collapsed patient, a team of doctors and nurses was quickly available to help me out. Here, I was entirely on my own.

"Will you please phone for an ambulance while I see to your wife?" I repeated in exasperation when I saw Albert was making no attempt to help me. I was desperately looking for a vein in Maggie's arm where I could put in a cannula. All her veins seemed to have collapsed.

Albert lowered his paper and glared at me, "She's not my wife, Griffin, she's my sister. Do your own phoning," and with a grunt of irritation he jerked his newspaper open and started to read.

I struggled to remain calm. What was I going to do? I glanced around the room and saw a timid, elderly lady sitting in a darkened corner, peering anxiously at me and Albert.

I beckoned to her gently, "Miss, could you please phone for an ambulance while I see to Maggie?"

She gave a hesitating glance towards Albert to make sure he didn't disapprove and, seeing no reaction, rushed off toward the phone. Albert carried on reading.

"That article you're reading, you great ignorant lout, must be the most interesting one ever written in the whole history of humanity." I thought to myself as I found a small vein.

Maggie was breathing but only just. I ran out to the Landrover and brought in an intravenous infusion set. I tried to find a dry patch in the enormous pool of blood that surrounded her where I could kneel down to insert the cannula into the vein I thought I felt in her arm.

Without thinking I reached over to Albert's heap of old newspapers and lifted one up to put under my knees to stop myself getting covered in blood. He jerked back as if I'd hit his thick neck with a baseball bat and bellowed, "Put that paper back, boy, I haven't read it yet."

I was so surprised I set the newspaper down again. Realising what I'd done, I snatched it up and said sharply, "You can read it after I've finished with it," and plonked it down on top of the matted blood.

Albert's face went as red as a fat strawberry. He looked so livid, I thought he was going to take a brain haemorrhage. I ignored him as I tried to insert a needle into Maggie's arm. I was elated at getting it in first time, I put up the intravenous infusion and ran in a litre of intravenous fluid. Maggie rallied slightly.

She had torn a varicose vein in her leg which had caused her to almost completely bleed to death.

Rupture of a varicose vein is not that common but when it occurs, the patient can lose a lot of blood in a very short time, though not usually as badly as in Maggie's case. It usually happens when an elderly person with varicose veins knocks their leg against a sharp object and splits the vein.

Dealing with it is simple and effective. All that needs to be done is find a large piece of material, like a towel or a blanket and press it firmly against the bleeding area and wait for the ambulance to arrive. The vein sometimes needs to be stitched in hospital if steady pressure doesn't stop it completely.

I tied a bandage around Maggie's leg over the torn vein and checked her blood pressure as I waited for the ambulance to arrive.

After what seemed an age, I heard the distant siren of an approaching ambulance. Albert never looked up or spoke the whole time.

Betty, the elderly lady who had phoned for the ambulance whispered she would make us all a nice cup of tea. I watched her collect some dirty looking cracked mugs from a grubby table before going into the kitchen. I listened to hear if there was any sound of washing up and didn't hear any. The thought of drinking out of Albert's dirty mug was too much for me.

When Betty came back in to take some lumpy sugar off a dresser, I took the opportunity to tell her as gently as I could that I never drank tea early in the morning. She looked crest fallen until I reassured her I felt sure the ambulance men would be delighted to have a nice cuppa after their long drive. That seemed to cheer her up.

The ambulance pulled into the back yard of the house and two ambulance men climbed out. One had a surly look about him and wouldn't speak to me. He looked like he had been wakened from his sleep and wasn't too pleased about it. I wondered if he and Albert were related.

Maggie had come round a little and was able to talk in a whisper. She thanked me as she was put on a stretcher and taken out to the ambulance. The surly ambulance driver came back in to gather up some of his equipment just as the tea arrived. I nodded to Betty to give him a mug as I slipped out of the door. I glanced at Albert. He was engrossed in a crossword and didn't look up.

Maggie made a slow recovery and returned home three weeks later.

Four months later when I told Dr Roberts about the incident with Albert and the newspaper, his eyes twinkled with delight.

"Albert," he said, "wouldn't you think with all his reading, he'd have learned something about manners?"

Dr Sylvester O'Flathertie

That first night in Slievegart was a baptism by fire.

When I returned from Albert's, I had a long soak in Dr Robert's enormous enamel bath and a cup of coffee from his specially imported Italian coffee making machine. I went outside into the sunshine filled garden to drink my coffee. Bonnie came over and lay down at my feet. The two sleek cats slunk over and sniffed about a bit before lazily settling themselves across Bonnie's back for a doze. There was something reassuring about their behaviour. It was as though they had accepted me into their household and into their community.

As I drank my coffee, I gazed across the bay at the trawlers returning from a night's fishing. They were all painted in sky blue or light yellow with dark red or white upper borders. One large dirty black trawler stood out. It lagged behind at the rear of the fleet. I wondered what sort of a man would captain an ugly boat like that.

Flights of seagulls soared and wheeled behind each boat waiting to plunge down for the tasty fish bits thrown overboard.

"I could get used to this part of General Practice," I thought to myself as I flicked open the morning paper. That was when the phone rang again.

"Oh no, not another call." I groaned. I raced inside to pick up the receiver.

A pleasant woman's voice spoke.

"Hello Doctor, I'm sorry to phone you so early in the morning. It's Mrs O'Shea speaking, I wanted to catch you before you started your morning surgery. I was wondering if you would be so kind as to call out some time and see my husband Charlie. He's hardly been out of his bed for the past three weeks and I'm getting worried about him."

"Certainly, Mrs O'Shea, I'll come round and see him straight after surgery today. Just give me your address." I was glad to oblige someone so agreeable, especially after my experience with Albert.

That morning's surgery was leisurely. It was a beautiful day and most of the villagers were busy fishing or bringing in the hay. A few regulars ambled in but a lot of them decided to wait and see Dr Roberts on his return.

In the afternoon I drove into the town and called at the O'Shea house. They lived in a terraced house facing the sea.

Mrs O'Shea was a motherly woman in her late thirties. I noticed her tired and worried appearance as she told me about her husband. Charlie was a fisherman. He had taken to his bed three weeks earlier and refused to speak or get up except to go to the bathroom.

The salmon season was about to start and, with it, a chance to earn some real money. Charlie was not interested. "Fish or no fish, I'm not a bit well," was all he would say if he spoke at all.

She showed me the way through the cramped house to the back bedroom where Charlie lay in bed. He was a huge, burly man who looked like he'd been squeezed into his bed with a shoe-horn. He was one of those awkward men you sometimes meet and wonder why any woman, ever married them. Charlie was sullen, morose and difficult.

His replies to my questions were monosyllabic and full of self pity. I took a detailed history and examined him thoroughly. He was as fit and strong a man as I'd ever seen. His appetite was prodigious and he slept like a log. I could find nothing to explain why he couldn't, or wouldn't get out of his bed for three weeks. Mrs O'Shea hovered anxiously in the doorway listening and watching silently as I examined her husband.

When I came out of the room I told her I couldn't find anything obviously wrong with Charlie but as she was so concerned, I would ask one of my colleagues to have a look at him the following day.

She looked relieved that something was being done until I mentioned I was going to consult Dr O'Flathertie. Her face clouded over.

"Is anything the matter, Mrs O'Shea?" I asked.

"Well, yes, sort of, Doctor. Charlie isn't too fond of Dr O'Flathertie."

"Is that so, Mrs O'Shea? That's a pity now because I understand from what Dr Roberts said Dr O'Flathertie is an excellent doctor."

"Well yes, Dr Griffin, Dr O'Flathertie is a great doctor but you see, it's like this, Charlie and Dr O'Flathertie haven't exactly got on very well in the past," Mrs O'Shea said hesitantly.

"Oh I see," I answered. "Did they have a bit of a disagreement?"

"They sort of did, Dr Griffin. We used to be on Dr O'Flathertie's list until one fine day, Dr O'Flathertie told Charlie that in his medical opinion, he thought Charlie was a big, ignorant, lazy, no good oaf of a man who needed a size fourteen boot to sort him out. Charlie has never felt the same about Dr O'Flathertie since."

I was taken aback by this gentle, ladylike woman's exact quoting of Dr O'Flathertie's words. It had obviously made a deep impression on her.

"I see," I said, wondering how I would get around this dilemma.

"What about if I bring Dr O'Flathertie along tomorrow without telling Charlie – just sort of tell him we're getting a second opinion."

She reluctantly agreed and I left wondering if Dr Robert's generous fee was worth all the work and trouble of the past 24 hours.

The next day I called at Dr O'Flathertie's home to ask him if he would come and see Charlie. He lived in a large white house with bright blue shutters. It was perched high on a rocky hill overlooking the sea. A beautifully kept lawn swept down towards Slievegart Bay. When I rang the doorbell, a tall distinguished man in his early fifties, wearing a tweed suit and a colourful cravat, answered the door. He took off his reading glasses to scrutinize me with an intensely quizzical look. When he heard who I was he welcomed me enthusiastically, delighted, as he put it, to have the opportunity to speak to a 'Medical Man who had recently left the great Learning Halls of Dublin'.

He offered me a glass of sherry as I gave him an outline of Charlie's history. Dr O'Flathertie peered intently at me over his half moon glasses as he poured himself a schoonerful.

When I finished he said, "Ah, Charlie O'Shea, an ignorant good for nothing if ever I met one. James, I know him well. Married to a lovely woman and eight beautiful children. Hardly provides for them at all and drinks the bit out. A glass of dry sherry wouldn't go too far with Charlie," he added as he downed his second schoonerful in a gulp.

He invited me to lunch and, after a meal of salmon caught that morning in Slievegart Bay and fresh vegetables from his own garden, Dr O'Flathertie lit a cigar and poured himself a generous glass of Hennessey brandy.

When I declined, 'le petit digestif', as Dr O'Flathertie put it, he said to me, "James me boy, you're going to wreck your digestion if you don't look after yourself. Brandy quells the gastric juices and invigorates the senses. It's just what a man like you needs in these trying circumstances."

I nodded in agreement, thinking if I'd drunk as much as he had in the past hour, I would be lying senseless on the floor. For the next half hour, Dr O'Flathertie entertained me with stories of his thirty years working around the world as a doctor. I began to look anxiously at the clock until he said, "James, you're not up in the big smoke now. The time in Slievegart is measured in days or weeks, not minutes. You'll have to slow yourself down to the pace of the locality or you'll never last it out here. This isn't St Vincent's Private Clinic you're dealing with now."

When he'd finished his cigar, he said, "We'll go down to see Charlie in my motor James, if you don't mind. I think it will be safer in the long run."

I wondered what on earth he meant by such a cryptic remark. I hadn't a chance to ask as he darted off to his garage.

I was expecting him to drive a Jaguar at least or possibly a Bentley. As he opened his garage door he revealed a blue, left-hand drive Deux Chevaux Citroen which he leapt into with surprising nimbleness. He drove it like a true Frenchman and, in those pre seatbelt days, I clung to the dash board as we careered into town. Within a matter of minutes, we screeched to a halt outside the O'Shea house.

He was out of the car and halfway up the drive before I had my door opened. Mrs O'Shea received us as graciously as a lady of the Manor. Despite that I sensed her anxiety. Dr O'Flathertie was charm personified. "Well now, how are you getting on at all, at all Mrs O'Shea? It's younger and better looking you're getting by the day. Where's that man of yours, Charles? Is he about the house at all? I'd like to see how he's getting on."

"He is, Dr O'Flathertie and I'm sorry to say he seems to be making heavy weather of his present condition."

"Is he now, Mrs O'Shea. Is he now?" Dr O'Flathertie clucked as he shook his head. "Well then, we'd better have a look at him. I'm sure we'll be able to sort something out." A look of relief passed over Mrs O'Shea's face as she turned to lead us to the back bedroom.

Charlie gave a grunt of irritation at seeing Dr O'Flathertie.

"Well how are you Charles, my old friend?" Dr O'Flathertie asked in his most affable manner as he stared at the recumbent figure. "I've never seen you looking so strong and healthy in all my days. I think by the look of you from this end of the bed you have a bad dose of the HAs but I'd better check you out just to be sure."

He pulled a stethoscope out from an inside pocket and listened attentively to Charlie's heart.

"Sound as a bell," he said after several minutes.

"Now, let's see how them lungs of yours are working." He applied the stethoscope to Charlie's back.

"Sound as two bells Charles. Isn't that the great news?"

Charlie looked crosser by the minute. After a prolonged examination of Charlie's mountainous abdomen, Dr O'Flathertie turned abruptly and said to Mrs O'Shea in a grave voice. "I need to have a word with you outside Mrs O'Shea. I think we have a bad case of the HAs here." We all trooped out leaving a suddenly very concerned Charlie, peering anxiously after us.

Dr O'Flahertie led the way to the living room where Mrs O'Shea's children were patiently waiting. He spoke somberly. "I can find nothing to suggest your husband has anything seriously wrong with him, Mrs O'Shea. He has the appetite of a ploughman. His heart is sound and if he could bray, his lungs would out bray the hind legs of any donkey in the whole of County Kerry. In my opinion he is suffering from nothing more sinister than a touch of the HAs."

"The HAs Dr O'Flahertie?"

"Yes, Mrs O'Shea, the HAs."

"And if you don't mind me asking, Dr O'Flahertie, could you please explain what the HAs are."

"The HAs, Mrs O'Shea, are the Hardly Ables as we medical men call them. There's a lot of it about. Hardly able to do this, hardly able to do that. Charlie has a bad dose of it."

Mrs O'Shea was taken aback by Dr O'Flahertie's diagnosis but after a moment or two, she breathed a sigh of relief.

"I wondered as much, Dr O'Flahertie. Do you think that's all that's wrong with him?"

"I do, Mrs O'Shea and I've known Charlie for more than twenty years."

The room was silent as the family digested this information. Eventually Charlie's wife spoke. "Charlie always was a bit on the lazy side Dr O'Flahertie. And to tell you the truth, I don't know what I'm going to do with him this time what with the salmon season just starting. It's the one time fishermen can earn a decent wage and we need the money with this crowd of young ones to rear. Is there anything you can do to cure him and get him out of his bed and back to work?"

Dr O'Flahertie looked thoughtful for a few moments before answering. "I know a way of getting Charlie out of his bed Mrs O'Shea. However, I must warn you, if I use this method, Charlie will not be himself for a few days. You might find him a little grumpy, angry even but he will be out of his bed and back at the fishing, I can guarantee you that. One other thing I ought to add is that if I do proceed, Charlie is unlikely to want to speak to me again for a very long time. With all that in mind, would you like me to go ahead?" I stood beside Dr O'Flathertie feeling completely lost, I looked from him to Mrs O'Shea and back to him.

It was the most bizarre clinical setting I have ever encountered. I didn't know what procedure Dr O'Flathertie had in mind and I was afraid to ask.

Mrs O'Shea and her children looked at each other. Then nodded their heads in agreement. At that signal, Dr O'Flathertie sprang into action. He lifted his medical bag and marching outside, put it in the boot of his car. He turned the car round so that the driver's door faced the house and, leaving the engine running, went back into the house. He stopped at the doorstep and looked at me intently. "Are you a good runner, James?" he asked.

"Fairly good," I answered perplexed.

"Well, James, you'd better be at your best today where the running is concerned," he continued enigmatically.

Without any further explanation, he went back into the house. As we moved towards Charlie's room, Dr O'Flathertie pushed aside some pieces of furniture.

"We don't want those in our way, do we?" he said to me with a smile.

I was feeling increasingly uneasy. This was new to me. I had never seen or heard of anything like this before as a medical student.

As we entered Charlie's bedroom, Dr O'Flathertie suddenly stopped. He spoke quietly, "Watch everything I do James, very closely. You're going to see something here today they don't teach in the great learning Halls of Dublin or even the great Universities of England and America combined – but you'll soon see, effective nonetheless. Now there's one thing you've got to remember James" and Dr O'Flathertie paused as he gripped my arm tightly and peered over his half moon glasses into my eyes.

"What's that?" I gulped.

"You must leave the bedroom as soon as I instruct you and jump into the passenger seat of the car. You must be as quick as you can. Remember it is essential you get into the passenger seat." As he repeated his advice, I saw a mischievous twinkle in his eye.

Before I could begin to think what was going to happen, Dr O'Flathertie strode purposefully into the bedroom with an air of supreme confidence.

Without a word, he threw back the bedclothes exposing Charlie's long, thick, hairy legs. Charlie peered uneasily at Dr O'Flathertie.

"I've come back to help you, Charlie me boy." Dr O'Flathertie said soothingly. "Listen well, Charlie, you may not like what I'm about to do and you may not thank me today or tomorrow or indeed for some time to come but you will eventually."

Charlie stared at Dr O'Flathertie like a moth mesmerized by a strong light. He seemed to relax under the spell of Dr O'Flathertie's hypnotic voice.

Suddenly Dr O'Flathertie, with a swift movement, grasped the back of Charlie's calf muscles with his long bony fingers.

He fixed his gaze on the inert Charlie and squeezed the muscles of his calves as hard as he could. The effect was dramatic. Charlie bellowed like an angry elephant and catapulted forward. With a deft movement that amazed me, Dr O'Flathertie tugged on Charlie's ankles, making the enormous man fall back into bed. He squeezed the muscles with renewed vigour.

Dr O'Flathertie repeated this process several times. Charlie groaned in pain and anger. Every time he tried to get up, Dr O'Flathertie tugged on his ankles, making him collapse back into his bed. Where did Dr O'Flathertie get the strength to make this bull of a man fall back like that?

After what seemed an age, Dr O'Flathertie turned to me, his brow beaded with perspiration and said, "Go to the car as quickly as you can James and don't delay." I needed little encouragement as I sprinted outside.

Moments after I reached the car, Dr O'Flathertie raced from the O'Shea household at a dignified trot and jumped into the driver's seat. He looked at me with a self-satisfied grin and then glanced towards the house where I saw a very angry looking Charlie limping painfully towards us. He had a big stick in his hand.

"What are you going to do now?" I blurted out when Dr O'Flathertie made no attempt to drive off. I was terrified Charlie would reach us before Dr O'Flathertie could get the car moving. Dr O'Flathertie looked at me with a glint in his eye. "We're going to take the advice Pope Clement's Doctor gave him as the Black Plague approached Rome in 1348."

"And what was that?" I stammered as I wondered frantically how we were ever going to get away before Charlie seriously injured us.

Dr O'Flathertie calmly noted the danger as Charlie lurched at the car with his stick. He put his foot to the floor and we accelerated away like a rocket off a launching pad.

When we were safely out of Charlie's reach, Dr O'Flathertie continued, "That doctor's advice James was 'Fuge Cito, Vade Longe, Rede Tarde'." He rolled out the Latin words in a loving cadence, "And that James means, 'Flee quickly, Go Far and Return Slowly'."

Charlie went back to his fishing. He never did speak to Dr O'Flathertie again. And I spent the rest of my time in Slievegart avoiding anyone who remotely resembled Charlie.

The Funeral

I needed a break from difficult patients and eccentric doctors after the O'Shea fiasco. Fortunately that Summer was the hottest in years. There was hardly a drop of rain in Slievegart during July and August. The good weather put people in great spirits and the attendance rate at the surgery was the lowest Hilda, the District Nurse, had ever seen in the thirty years she had worked there.

The villagers got up late and went to bed late. There was no point opening the surgery before 10 am. The only early riser in the village was a French man called Yves, who had married a local girl. He ran a bakery and delicatessen and sold apricot jam and croissants long before they were freely available in Dublin. Yves had the people of Slievegart conversant with the subtleties of blue cheese and baguettes before their city cousins had ever heard of them.

Each morning at ten o'clock I would amble into the surgery full of café latte and fresh French croissants. One or two patients would be in the waiting room, chatting about the great spell of weather or the price of salmon.

The patients were easy going and friendly. I found it hard to understand them at first as they spoke so quickly and quietly. There were no appointments and patients strolled in as they pleased. If there were too many in the waiting room for their liking, they went out again and came back the following day or the day after that.

When the surgery closed for the morning, I would have a cup of tea with Hilda and hear the local news, before doing the home visits, if there were any. These visits were usually up into the mountains to old people who were not fit to travel or to those who were unable to get to the surgery.

I was always glad if there was a call up into the mountains. I loved an excuse to drive the Landrover through the narrow roads that wound their way into the heather covered hills. There was almost no traffic. Because they were used so infrequently, the roads had a band of grass that grew down the middle. Sheep wandered everywhere and I had to drive slowly to avoid them. They sometimes lay down on the road and refused to get up even if I honked the horn. I had to get out and chase them down the road. I would often go round the next corner and find more of them lying down.

In many ways the sheep reflected the area and the people who lived in it. They had no understanding of the words hurry or urgent. There was a timelessness and contentment and an easy goingness that made me slow down from the frenetic pace of life I had been used to as a student and junior doctor.

The higher I drove into the hills, the quieter it was. There would be no sound other than the distant rumble of the sea and the occasional cry of a curlew. I sometimes got out of the Landrover and looked down at the surf crashing against the side of a cliff or onto a beach four hundred feet below.

On a sunny day, with the breeze coming in from the sea and the tang of salt in the air, I often lay down in the long grass at the side of the road and gazed up at the blue sky. Far below I would hear the Atlantic Ocean. I understood then what an old mountain man meant when he once said to me.

"Sometimes, I wake up and go out my front door first thing in the morning as the sun rises. I look across yonder to them green hills and down onto that rolling sea. I think then I've died in my sleep and woken up in paradise."

The mountain people were a breed apart. They were sturdy, silent people, with a natural graciousness I had never witnessed before. They spoke in a soft brogue which was almost musical. I sometimes asked them questions just to hear them speak.

Most of them lived in small, white washed cottages which were thatched and faced the sea. The windows were small to keep out the storm winds that blew in from the Atlantic in the winter months. As you approached each house, the welcoming smell of burning turf greeted you. Every house had a stack of turf packed several yards away from the front door. The stack was built with great skill to keep the inner sods dry from the rain. They were barn shaped and narrowed as they got higher. Some of the stacks were nearly as big as the cottages.

The main room was the sitting room and off it were two bedrooms. If there was a large family, the older children slept in a loft above the kitchen which they approached by climbing a ladder. There was a turf fire on in the kitchen all through the year and that kept the loft warm.

Some of the old people slept in what was called the cul leabra (corner bed) – a long wooden seat beside the fire that doubled as a bed at night.

All the floors were made of stone and had hay and cow dung below them to act as insulation. This was long before the days of plastic insulation Some of the houses higher in the mountains had no electricity. They used Tilley lamps at night that gave off heat as well as light.

If it wasn't raining the doors of the cottages were left open all summer to let light in. Small children were stopped from running outside and falling off a cliff by closing the lower part of the door (called a half door). You would often see the woman of the house leaning on the half door as she talked to a passer by. Old men sat outside the cottages smoking their pipes and chatting softly.

I often felt I had gone back to another age, to a gentle place where life was as it should be.

In the afternoon, if all was quiet, I ambled through the village or swam in the sea and rested in the sun before going back for the lacksadaisical evening surgery.

Night calls were rare, unlike the first unforgettable night. After six weeks of this idyllic life, I felt as though I had been in Slievegart a lifetime. I half wished I could have stayed there for the rest of my life.

A phone call one morning to visit an elderly man after the morning surgery made me think again. The man I was asked to see was an eighty six year old called Anton Mor which, in English, means Big Anthony.

Anton Mor had 'taken bad'. He had never been ill in his life before. For the past three months he had been losing weight and becoming increasingly weak. He now had difficulty getting out of bed in the mornings.

I called that afternoon to see him in his isolated cottage high up in the Kerry Mountains. He met me at the door. He had a natural grace and kindliness about him that made me like him immediately. He was what we call in Ireland, 'one of nature's gentlemen'.

I talked to him for a short while and explained I needed to examine him. He went off to lie down in his bedroom and while I waited for him to change, I chatted to his wife, Kitty. Even at eighty years of age, she had a beautiful, kindly face.

Kitty told me she and Anton Mor has been married sixty years and that he was the best man any woman could ever have married. She said she had never heard him complain about anything in his life.

If six of his sheep died or if his dinner was burnt or if the best plate in the house was broken, all he would ever say was, "That's the will of God, Kitty, that must be what He wants." On occasion she said she had exploded with anger at his complacency and his acceptance of all eventualities. Anton Mor would only laugh at her and say, "I love the fire you have in you Kitty. It's the reason I married you." He would put his arm around her and whisper softly to her until she calmed down.

Lately she had noticed him clutching his stomach and wincing several times a day. His appetite, which had been prodigious, was greatly reduced. If she asked him what was wrong he would only say, "There's not a bother on me Kitty and if it wasn't for this old arthritis I'd be galloping over those hills again like a young 'un."

I examined Anton Mor in his bedroom and was upset to find he had a massive hard growth in his abdomen. I knew at once he had some form of advanced cancer and that his days were numbered. I hated the thought of having to tell Kitty the bad news.

Anton Mor had ten grown up children and several of them had gathered that day outside the house when they heard the doctor was coming to examine their greatly loved father.

When I came out of the bedroom I told Kitty and the family as gently as I could that Anton Mor was ill and needed to go to Tralee Hospital for further investigations. Kitty began to cry. Through her tears she sobbed, "You know, Doctor, Anton Mor has never left Slievegart since he came home from the trenches of the Great War in 1918. He told me many times since then that after all he'd been through, he'd seen enough of the world to do him and he'd never leave his own village again.

As she spoke, tears flowed down her lovely face. One of her big sons came over and put his arm around her shoulders.

"Come on mother," he said soothingly. "Don't be crying now, the Doctor might be able to help Anton Mor yet if he'll do what he's told. What do you think Doctor? Does he need to go to Tralee Hospital?" he asked as he turned towards me.

I was torn between saying, "They might be able to do something for your father," and what I really believed, "Your father will be dead within the month, whether he goes to Tralee or not." I didn't want to make them lose all hope but I didn't know with my inexperience at the time, what was the right answer.

I looked round at his sons and daughters and said, "What would you like me to do for your father? I could look after him here or if you prefer I could get him moved to hospital and see if there is anything more that can be done for him there. I'll leave you to discuss it between yourselves." I went outside and, as I waited, I looked down the mountain at the beautiful view of the sun shining warmly over the bay of Slievegart.

The family talked quietly amongst themselves and after some time told me they had decided they would like Anton Mor to be investigated in Tralee. I went back in to see him. He lay on his bed, his eyes closed, as he quietly prayed the Rosary, his fingers moving slowly over the beads. I told him he wasn't in a great condition and needed to go into hospital to see if anything could be done to help him. I added, "You know Mr O'Sullivan, your family are keen for you to be investigated in Tralee."

He looked at me with his honest blue eyes, "Doctor," he said, "I'm dying and I know it. My time has come. I know it and I know you know it. It's about time that lot out there knew it as well and accepted it – but they won't. They'll be looking for miracles. I haven't long left and there's nothing anybody can do for me – but I suppose if it'll keep them happy, I'll go to Tralee."

He spoke with no self pity and a gentle resignation. I was moved by his tremendous generosity of spirit. I shook his hand without speaking as I thought, "Here's an old man tired out and about to die and all he wants is to spend his remaining days at home without any fuss yet he agrees to go to hospital to keep his family happy."

Two hours later he left by ambulance for Tralee. When I phoned the hospital the next day the surgeon told me Anton Mor had a massive inoperable stomach cancer with secondaries spread throughout his body. He was surprised the man was still alive and put it down to him having such a strong constitution from running up and down mountains herding sheep and cattle all his life.

He said they were going to let him go home to die in three or four days time, after they had built him up with some intravenous nutrition.

The next day I was stunned to be phoned by the Ward Sister, and told that Anton Mor had died the previous evening. She said his wife had been holding his hand when he turned and smiled at her, "Kitty, a gra mo chroi (love of my heart)," he whispered, "I have always loved you and I always will." He squeezed her hand gently and putting his head back, died as quietly as he had lived.

I called at the house that evening as the sun was setting. Many people had come from miles around to pay their last respects to so fine a man. Anton Mor had no enemies and everyone regarded him as a friend. I followed one of his sons

34

who had come to greet me through the throngs of people into their house and found Kitty sobbing quietly beside the fire. She shook my hand warmly and thanked me for all my help. She said Anton Mor was the best man she had ever known and that she was privileged to have been the wife of such a man for so many years. I was touched by her kindness and only wished I had insisted that the poor man stay at home and die in his own bed, instead of getting him to make that long futile journey to Tralee. His sons came over and thanked me as well. They were all big strong men like their father and had his stoical demeanor.

"It was for the best Doctor," one of them said to me. "Anton Mor had a long life and he died peacefully with my mother beside him. She was everything to him. That's all he would have wanted, Kitty by his side, holding his hand. Wasn't it better he died like that rather than after a long drawn out illness? God was good to him letting him die so."

One of his daughters, Annie, brought me over a cup of tea and as is custom at Irish wakes, sat beside me and talked about the person who had died.

"You know Doctor," she said, "My father had a great love of words and stories. He was a kind of a bard and storyteller here-abouts. Words and poetry were music to him. He used to tell us when we were children and indeed, all our lives that he loved us, each and every one of us. He often said to me especially as he grew older, 'Now my little Annie darling, you're to promise me one thing. When I die you are to make sure these words are put on my gravestone.' And Annie spoke those words softly.

'I gave my heart to Kitty O'Donnell the day I met her,
I'll give my soul to God the moment I meet him
And the rest I give back to Slievegart.'

"He was a wonderful man and father, doctor and I like to think he's already handed his soul over to God." I went back home that night edified by the dignity and strength of the man and his family.

However, life in General Practice is rarely straightforward. The following morning in the middle of surgery, I got a phone call from one of Anton Mor's sons. He sounded agitated and upset. He asked me to call at the house as soon as possible.

"What's the matter?" I asked. "Is your mother not well?"

"She's very, very upset Doctor. The Gardai have arrived up here and they want to take my father's body back to Tralee for a post mortem."

"A post mortem," I gasped. I could hardly believe my ears. "What on earth for?"

"We don't know doctor and would greatly appreciate it if you would come up and sort things out for us as soon as you can. My mother's in an awful state"

I made my excuses at the surgery and left immediately. When I arrived at the house I saw three uneasy red-faced policemen and a pompous looking Sergeant with a huge stomach hanging over his thick policeman's belt, standing at the door of the O'Sullivan house. They were surrounded by the six tall O'Sullivan men who looked very angry.

The Sergeant turned around when he heard the doctor had arrived. He wasn't a bit pleased when he saw me. "Where's Dr Roberts?" he whispered urgently to one of his Constables. He was one of those men who are incapable of speaking quietly or hiding their feelings. His whispering boomed out, almost across the valley.

The embarrassed Constable muttered that Dr Roberts was on prolonged leave and I was his replacement. The Sergeant raised his eyes to heaven. "The very time you need that boyo Roberts, he's not here and when you don't want him he's never out of your road. Would you look at that brainless looking young sidekick he's left to look after things at a time like this."

"Well doctor," he said to me in his official voice, as he stepped towards me, unaware I'd heard every word he'd said. "We have a rare and quare situation here, a most discombobulating and contumacious situation I have to say. The County Coroner for Kerry has instructed me to proceed forthwith to the abode of the deceased, one Anthony O'Sullivan, known in the Irish as Anton Mor O'Suilleabhan, and to remove his remains to the Tralee Mortuary whence a post mortem is to be undertaken, sub-judice, to determine the cause of death."

"Why can't you speak like someone half sensible, instead of that pretentious legalistic jargon?" I thought angrily to myself, as the Sergeant warmed to his task. He seemed oblivious to the consternation his presence had evoked.

I glanced round and saw the O'Sullivan men looked as if they were prepared to defend the removal of their father's remains with their lives, if necessary. I knew I'd have to do my best to control my own annoyance and calm things down for everyone's sake.

"And why does Mr O'Sullivan need a post mortem?" I asked the Sergeant. "The cause of his death is well known. I spoke to the Surgeon in the hospital myself two days ago and to the Ward Sister only yesterday and they both told me he had advanced stomach cancer."

"The exact cause of Mr O'Sullivan's untimely and abstruse death is not known Doctor," the Sergeant said with relish. "The cause of Mr O'Sullivan's death is indeed very uncertain."

"But the Surgeon himself told me ..."

The Sergeant interrupted ponderously, "It has come to light Doctor, that the cause of Mr O'Sullivan's death may have been other than by natural means."

"What do you mean, by other than natural means, Sergeant?" I asked, totally perplexed.

"The cause of death may have been occasioned by perfidious foul play."

"Foul play?" I gasped.

A murmur spread like a tidal wave through the crowd.

"Yes indeed, foul play," the Sergeant repeated slowly, savouring every word. He was enjoying this moment of drama, with himself the centre of attention.

"What sort of foul play are you talking about Sergeant?" I asked.

"By foul play, I mean a rancorous blow to the head."

There was an intake of breath from the onlookers as Sergeant Murphy's voice thundered out. The pedantic Sergeant Murphy with his ridiculous accusations was beginning to irritate me intensely. "How could an old man lying in bed, dying and holding his wife's hand, have been killed by a blow to the head?" I asked. "It sounds both impossible and ludicrous."

"It is neither impossible nor ludicrous," the Sergeant said, rolling out the word ludicrous with relish, savouring every syllable. as though he was biting into a ripe peach. "It is highly probable Mr O'Sullivan was murdered by a mighty thump to the cranium."

"Murdered?" I said in amazement. Another gasp of astonishment and excitement swept through the crowd.

"Yes indeed, murdered," the Sergeant said emphatically, enjoying more by the minute the furore he was creating. "That is why a post mortem has to be undertaken Doctor – to rule out foul play or indeed murder."

"Is this daft Sergeant saying Mr O'Sullivan was murdered as he lay dying?" I asked myself. It was too outrageous to even contemplate.

"Are you suggesting Sergeant Murphy, that Mr O'Sullivan could have been murdered as he lay dying with his wife beside him and she wouldn't have noticed anything?" I asked.

"It is not within my jurisdiction to comment on the deceased wife's powers of observation regarding the cause or causes of the deceased's passing, that is a decision which the State Pathologist will have to arrive at and himself alone in his professional capacity. All I can say at this given time, with the information that is presently available to me, it is a possibility and the reason henceforth for a post mortem."

"Who is alleged to have struck the fatal blow to Mr O'Sullivan's head Sergeant?" I asked, realizing, to my irritation, I had lapsed into the Sergeants ridiculous form of officialdom speech.

"A gentleman from another ward of the hospital, Doctor, I am only permitted to say, given the confines and confidentiality of my post. A gentleman suffering from an undisclosed condition, was seen the morning of the deceased's death to be in proximity to the deceased's bed. It is understood this gentleman may have struck the deceased on the side of the head with a heavy implement causing his subsequent demise."

"A heavy implement, Sergeant?" I asked, bewildered.

"Indeed doctor, a heavy implement."

"What sort of heavy implement are you talking about Sergeant?" I asked.

"A bottle of Lucozade," he replied.

"A bottle of Lucozade, Sergeant?" I repeated in disbelief.

"Yes indeed doctor, a half full or indeed, a half empty bottle of that aforementioned mephitic solution."

"Did anyone see this alleged assault?"

"A member of staff was reported to have seen the assault."

"What member of staff Sergeant?" I persisted.

"The member of staff wishes their identity to remain undisclosed. They wish to remain incognito at this present moment."

"Incognito?"

"Yes, Doctor, incognito. In-cog-nit-o" he repeated slowly, his eyes closed. He loved that word. It was like music to his ears.

I saw I couldn't turn the Sergeant from his path. To him the law was the law, right or wrong. If the Coroner had told him to arrest his own mother on suspicion of having killed Anton Mor, he would have proceeded forthwith with due caution to her abode and arrested her, having warned her of her rights before dragging her from her nursing home.

Come hell or high water, Mr O'Sullivan was going to have a post mortem whether or not he needed it, as far as Sergeant Murphy was concerned.

After much heated discussion, the family agreed to the post mortem. The Undertaker was summoned and the coffin of Anton Mor was put back into the hearse amidst many tears. The large crowd of mourners stood silently by as the six sons carried their fathers coffin out of his house to the hearse.

The funeral had been arranged for the following day in the village Chapel but now had to be postponed until after the post mortem. As the hearse drove slowly down the hillside, one of Anton Mor's neighbours, a man called Jimmy Johnny, turned to me and whispered earnestly, "Do you think Doctor, he'll be back in time for his funeral?"

It was the most extraordinary question I'd ever been asked. I didn't know whether to laugh at its absurdity or be touched by its pathos. But I knew, in the end, I was going to laugh - and laugh a lot.

As I stood and mulled over Jimmy Johnny's query I felt a surge in my throat I suppressed with difficulty. I had to leave immediately before the full impact of Jimmy Johnny's question hit me. Sad Irish wakes are not the place to burst into wild laughter.

I quickly shook hands with some of the family who were standing nearby and keeping my head down mumbled, in a choking voice, I'd call again after the funeral.

I moved briskly down the garden path hoping the onlookers wouldn't notice my shoulders shaking. I jumped into the Landover and letting the handbrake off, rolled down the hill. Only then did I start to laugh, laughing in gales, until the tears came to my eyes and the tension swept away, a mixture of many emotions.

As I laughed I thought of how Anton Mor would have appreciated the irony of being late for his own funeral. I imagined him throwing back his noble head and laughing exuberantly and the wind tossing his laughter back into the wind rushed hills of the Kerry mountains.

The post mortem showed death by natural causes. Anton Mor was laid to rest two days later in the silence of his own Churchyard. Yes, he was back in time for his funeral – the biggest ever seen in Slievegart.

And as for poor Kitty, she just couldn't go on without her Big Anthony. When I went to see her a week after the funeral, I was shocked by how badly she had gone downhill in so short a time. She had become an old, old woman. She told me then she hadn't long to live. "Anton Mor is waiting for me Doctor. I can feel him beckoning and I can't wait to see him again. I miss him more than life itself." Two weeks later, Kitty died peacefully in her sleep. Her coffin was laid alongside her husband's in Slievegart cemetery, amidst many tears.

Father Jeremiah O'Donovan, the kindly old parish priest summed it all up at the graveside. "Kitty has gone to her home in heaven for ever and ever, to be with the two people she loved with all her heart and with all her soul – God and Anton Mor."

All at Sea

After the anger of Albert, the shenanigans of Charlie and the sadness of Kitty and Anton Mors' death, I needed something to relax me so I could face the challenges of the following day…. I found it by taking Bonnie for a walk every evening down to the sea. We would visit the harbour first and then go for a long walk along the beach and over the sand dunes. The more I took Bonnie walking, the more attached we became to each other.

In the evening when I came out of the surgery, she would be waiting by the door and leap to her feet, her tail wagging furiously. She'd let out yelps of impatience as I went off to change my clothes.

"Bonnie'll never look at Dr Roberts again when he gets back after the way you've spoilt her." Hilda used to say to me which pleased me enormously. I always loved dogs, especially Labradors and Retrievers I had found the way to a dog's heart is not through its stomach but through its feet and long walks.

Bonnie and I would start by strolling down the hill from Dr Robert's house to look at the fishing boats tied up in the harbour. I loved the sea and somehow, looking at the peaceful scene in the early evening banished all the worries of the day from my mind.

However distant doctors may seem to the patient, they often bring their work home with them and I was beginning to find that out early in my career. Looking at the colourful fishing boats against the fading light of the evening sky helped me to put everything in context.

My family originally came from Donegal on the north west coast of Ireland. They had been fishermen for generations. Love of the sea must have been in my blood or so I liked to think. Every evening I would feel an irresistible urge to go and see the fishing trawlers preparing for a night on the water. I loved everything about them, the bustle of the fishermen tidying their nets or scrubbing the decks, the smell of fish, the lapping of the waves against the hulls, the seagulls calling as they wheeled overhead as if they, too, were excited at the prospect of a night's fishing all added to the atmosphere.

The trawlers were brightly coloured. They were painted in sky blue or soft yellow with red or green gunwales and named after saints. There was St. Naoimh, St. Brigid, St. Anne and my favourite, The Sancta Maria. It was a beautiful boat painted light blue with white gunwales.

There was one that was different from the others. It was painted black and looked completely out of place. It was owned by Charlie O'Shea. I was careful to avoid that boat whenever I walked along the harbour. It was aptly named The Black Bull. I couldn't have given it a better name myself, though on reflection, The Raging Donkey might have been more appropriate as thoughts of him jumping out of bed and roaring after Dr O'Flahertie came to mind.

One evening when I was wandering along the harbour, pausing from time to time to breathe in the sea air and absorb the serenity of the scene, I met the skipper of The Sancta Maria beside his boat.

"Well hello there, Doc. Out walking the dog again I see" Phil Ban greeted me, "Do you know you're the very man I'm looking for."

My heart sank.

It's the one thing a G.P. dislikes, getting caught by a patient when off duty and looking forward to a quiet walk or watching a football match.

"My Granny's constipation is killing her, doc. Could you call round on your way home to see her," they would say.

"I'm on my way to a match...."!

"Could you call in after the match then?"

It's difficult to smile or look interested in circumstances like that.

It wasn't like Phil Ban Sweeney to complain. He was a tough fisherman and ran the best trawler in the fleet. It was always spick and span. I'd heard a man say Phil Ban's boat was so clean you could have eaten your dinner off the deck.

Phil Ban, in his white peaked Captain's cap and Aran sweater looked like a man who was used to giving orders. He was broad and stocky with a mop of sun bleached hair that fell over his tanned face. His twinkling, blue eyes suggested he looked at the world with humour. He was known as Phil Ban because of his almost white hair (White Phil).

"Well, Phil Ban," I said, "what's the problem. Are you not feeling well?"

"I've never felt better in my entire life, doc," he said taking his briar pipe from his mouth. "It's that brother of mine, Jim, home from New York. It's him that's the problem."

"Is he not well?"

"Ah, he's well enough although I don't know how he can be. He should be dead the way he eats and drinks and him a diabetic on insulin."

"Well then, what's the problem?"

"I'll tell you what the problem is, Doc. My brother's an old fool who should grow up at his time of life and catch himself on. Do you know what he wants to do? He wants to come out on the boat with me for a night's fishing and him sixty seven years old. He's insisting on going tonight."

"What's wrong with that Phil. I know a lot of people who would jump at the chance of doing the same" and I was thinking, there's one standing here right in front of you. "You've a big boat and plenty of berths where he can lie down if he feels sea sick."

"It's not the seasickness that worries me, Doc. The old eejit thinks he has the sea legs of a buccaneer anyway even though he hasn't been on a boat since he left these shores for the Big Apple nearly fifty years ago. It's his diabetes I'm worried about. I'm worried it could go haywire when we're fifteen miles out to sea, I wouldn't know what to do if he went into a diabetic coma or something like that. He's been in comas before with low blood sugar and nearly died twice but it doesn't seem to bother him in the slightest. To tell you the truth, I don't know how his blood sugar could have gone down with the amount he eats. That's what has me worried, I'd like someone like yourself on the boat tonight, to keep an eye on him. I need someone to put my mind at rest and keep Big Jim right so I can get on with my job. Is there any chance you could spare the time to come with us?"

Could I spare the time? I could hardly keep the excitement out of my voice as I told him I would be delighted to go. It was a chance in a thousand. I had watched the trawlers set out each evening and return with the first light of dawn. I had often thought how much I would have loved to be going with them and wondered what it would be like to be on the open sea.

"Are you serious?" Phil asked. He sounded delighted.

"Of course I'm serious. I'd love to go. I'm not on duty, the sea's calm and you've the best boat in Kerry. I'd be very happy to go out with you."

"Well thanks a million Doc, thanks a million indeed. You're a real life saver. You've put my mind completely at rest. I owe you one." Phil Ban said enthusiastically as he shook my hand for nearly a minute.

I rushed back to get some warm clothes. I knew only too well from the night calls I had made over the last few weeks, how cold the nights could become. As I hurried back to the harbour, I thought of the time my father had fancied a similar trip. He had asked the skipper of a trawler to take him for a night's fishing off the west coast of Donegal.

"But Paddy," my mother had said with alarm, "You'll be as sick as a parrot. You know how you even get car sick if we don't keep stopping and you can't keep stopping in the middle of the Atlantic Ocean. The forecast for tonight is dreadful too, strong winds and storms. How do you think you'll manage with twenty foot waves crashing over your head? You'll not be able to stand it."

"Ah, don't talk nonsense, Joan. I only get car sick on rare occasions when the car's too hot and stuffy. There'll be no problem with stuffiness tonight ten miles beyond Aran Mor, not with that wind from the Atlantic. I'll be as right as rain."

My mother tried to dissuade him but he wouldn't listen. She told him he'd leave her a widow and the children fatherless.

"You'll be no widow," he retorted, "I'll be back in the morning with a barrel full of salmon for all of you."

She might as well have tried to turn the tide like King Canute as change his mind. He set off in the trawler that evening in great spirits. He said he felt so good he started to sing. I doubt if the crew would have appreciated that. He was tone deaf.

When they got beyond Aran Mor Island, they came into the full force of the Atlantic swell and it was a cold and blustery night. It was a long time afterwards my father told me what happened.

"It was all going along very nicely at the start James. I was thinking I had the sea legs of Admiral Nelson himself as we left the harbour and sailed into what I thought was the open sea but we were still only in a cove. Things seemed to take a turn for the worse even then. The swells were six to eight feet high and I began to feel a bit queasy, I thought I could put up with it and I didn't say anything but once we went past the north end of Aran Mor Island, we were into the open Atlantic. There was 3,000 miles of ocean then and nothing to break the waves. They hit the boat like a train.

Suddenly there were waves fifteen and twenty feet high bearing down on us and crashing over the deck. I held on like grim death expecting to be swept overboard at any moment. Nobody had life jackets in those days and I began to think there wasn't a chance of my surviving.

The crew went about their business as if they were taking a stroll in the park. I was terrified and feeling sicker by the moment. I started to vomit and I brought up everything I'd ever eaten from the day and hour I was born. After that, I started dry retching and that was ten times worse. My head started to spin and I had difficulty standing up.

I staggered downstairs and fell into a bunk but it was worse down there with the stink of stale fish and diesel oil and body odours. The boat rolled and tossed me about as if I was a rubber doll. I held on as long as I could but it only got worse. I thought I was going to die. I staggered up to the cabin where the captain was steering. He was smoking a pipe and looking at the sea completely unconcerned about the dreadful storm brewing up. You would have thought he was sailing a model boat on a duck pond, he was that content..

The smell of his pipe made me feel worse and I started retching again. I was as green as bile. The captain looked at me.

"Your face is green doc. It's actually pure green. It's as green as a child's snot," he said in amazement. He was gobsmacked. "It's the first time I've ever seen anybody with a green face. I've heard tell about people with green faces from seasickness but I've never seen one before myself."

"I'm happy for you," my father managed to say, "but that's not actually why I'm here. I'm going to die if this storm goes on much longer."

"Storm," he exclaimed, "storm? What storm are you talking about?"

"This storm and these waves, that's what I'm talking about. They're making me as sick as a dog."

"Oh, that'll pass," he said dismissively plugging that vile pipe of his back into his mouth. "That's not a storm at all, it's only a bit of a squall."

"It might be a squall to you, skipper, but it's the worst weather I've ever experienced in my entire life. I've got to get back to dry land or I'll never last the night."

"Not a chance, Doc. We couldn't go back now. We'd lose a night's fishing and I'd still have to pay the men their wages."

By that time I was so desperate, I'd have done nearly anything to get off the boat. I told him I'd pay whatever the night's fishing would have been as long as he turned round and got me back to Burtonport harbour. He agreed but he was very reluctant. The crew were delighted though. They had a night's pay for three hours work. That suited them fine.

My father got home in the early hours of the morning and told my mother he had changed his mind about going on the fishing trip. I don't think she ever did find out about the huge cheque he had to write.

I pushed the details of my father's trip to the back of my mind as I returned to the pier, muffled in a wool sweater and carrying a heavy overcoat. Phil Ban grabbed my hand and shook it until I thought my arm was loosening. He beamed with delight and told me over and over how relieved he was. He looked as though he had just won the sweepstakes.

"Thanks a million again, Doc," he said, "you've no idea what a relief it is you being here, you've taken a ton weight off my mind. I'll go and find Big Jim. You can have a word with him but don't expect too much co-operation or sense from him. He's an impossible man to tie down about anything."

Phil went off down the pier to look for his brother. He didn't have to go far. Big Jim had disappeared into the Harbour Bar. Phil came back a few minutes later accompanied by a big man who looked like an enormous, sulky teddy bear whose pot of honey had just been stolen (Big Jim didn't like having his pint of stout interrupted) but when he smiled his whole face lit up. He looked so happy and jolly then that as soon as anyone met him, they started to smile too.

"Well, well, well," he said coming up to me and holding out a massive hand to shake mine, "if it isn't the doctor himself, the man that's going to keep me alive tonight out on the high seas while Shorty here drives the boat."

He nodded towards his younger brother. He had a soft Kerry accent with a slight American twang. You couldn't help but take a liking to the man and it was obvious that Phil Ban, despite all his 'old fool' talk was very fond of Big Jim and Big Jim was fond of him.

"Well now, " he went on before I had a chance to say a word, "the Kerry fleet sails in an hour, at nine o'clock to be precise and I need to go and pack my teddy bear and pyjamas. I suppose you'll have to do the same, Doc so we'd better be off and see to it."

He turned round and ambled straight back to the Harbour Bar. Phil looked at me and raised his eyes to heaven.

We set sail an hour later and we nearly left without Big Jim. He came waddling up the pier at three minutes to the hour singing Percy French songs and looking like a happy schoolboy on an outing.

"Ahoy there me hearties," he shouted as he stumbled aboard. Look lively and cast her off. Take this vessel out into the big deep."

Big Jim was irrepressible. He kept everyone in stitches with his ridiculous comments including Phil Ban who tried hard to be serious and concentrate on his job. Every so often, Big Jim would take an enormous hip flask from his pocket and offer it round to everybody before drinking deeply from it himself.

"That whiskey you're drinking Jim, can't be too good for your diabetes," I tried saying diplomatically the first time he took a swig. "It'll send it haywire it and lower your blood sugar."

"No, no, you're all wrong there, Doc. It's not bad for my diabetes at all," he retorted. "Whiskey is good for it. I lower the blood sugar with whiskey and bring it back up again with a great big fry-up. I've the whole thing under control with all the years of practice I've put into it. I know more about controlling diabetes than any doctor ever will"

I understood why Phil Ban had been worried. Big Jim looked as though he could present me with a very tricky medical deliemma. It suddenly struck me. What would I do if this giant of a man went into a diabetic coma on a rough sea twenty miles from land? Maybe I would have been better just taking the dog for a longer walk.

I put those dark thoughts behind me as we sailed out towards the setting sun on a warm, balmy night. The stars were beginning to twinkle in a darkening sky. It felt more like being in the Caribbean than off the coast of West Kerry. The setting sun cast a long band of orange light over the glassy sea as we chugged out to the fishing grounds. Every thirty seconds or so there would be a peal of laughter as Big Jim made another wisecrack.

I looked back past the white wake of the boat to the receding coastline. There was a haze over the Kerry mountains and shadows in the hills. The lights of Slievegart town twinkled in the dusk. There was a stillness in the air and a silence that was almost mystical. I heard the crew laugh at another of Big Jim's jokes but it was a muffled sound that hardly pierced the silence. I seemed, for several magical moments, to be at peace with the world and all mankind. It was one of the happiest moments of my life. It wasn't to last.

Two hours later, we reached the fishing grounds. It was an unusually calm night. A full moon shone in the sky making the sea silver. There was hardly a wave to be seen. It was like being in the middle of a huge pond. The fishermen weren't happy with the weather.

"It's about the worst weather possible for fishing," Phil Ban explained. I could see he was disgruntled. Even Big Jim had gone quiet. "A calm sea and a bright moon is about the worst combination for fishing, bar a storm. The fish can see the nets. There's not much wind tonight so at least we can turn off the engines to keep the noise down and not frighten the fish away."

I was overawed by the silence and the enormous expanse of sea but, after a few minutes, my awe began to be replaced by a feeling of nausea. The boat was gently bobbing up and down like a cork in a bath as it drifted on the tiny swells. It was a constant movement that seemed to roll my stomach from side to side.

After a few minutes of mounting nausea, I rushed to the side of the boat and was violently sick. The smoked mackerel I'd had for supper found itself unexpectedly returned to the sea. I began to vomit and vomit and I wondered if I was ever going to stop. I didn't think my stomach could hold so much and I was cross with myself for being greedy and eating a second mackerel. Now I was paying the price for my greed.

"Having a bit of trouble with the stomach, Doc?" Big Jim said sympathetically, "a boat drifting in a sea like this is harder on the stomach than any stormy weather. It never gives it a moment's peace".

I could see a couple of the young crew laughing at my discomfort but I was past caring. I could never remember feeling so ill in my life. I was retching and retching. My head was spinning and I had difficulty standing upright. The world seemed to be rotating too fast. I didn't know how I could endure this terrible feeling of sickness until the morning. I had visions of myself having to write out a big cheque like my father and leave myself completely bankrupt.

A short while later, one of the young fishermen came over with a glass. He was grinning from ear to ear. "Here, drink this down doc. It'll settle your stomach in a second or two," he said

"What is it?" I asked. I didn't entirely trust his grin.

"Alka Seltzer," he said, "the best thing in the world for sea sickness. "Will you drink it or will I throw it into the sea?"

"I'll drink it alright, if it will help."

"It will help the very best though by the look on your face, doc, I'd say you'd drink the sweat from a camel's armpit if you thought it would ease you now." He and the rest of the crew laughed hysterically at that comment.

I felt bad but I don't know if I felt that bad. I had my dignity to think of after all. Camel sweat indeed!

I gulped the Alka Seltzer back and, almost immediately, I felt as though my stomach was gripped in a vice. I gave an almighty heave and the rest of the mackerel joined what I had already restored to the sea. I felt a lot better after that although I was still a bit dizzy.

The young fishermen laughed uproariously. The one who had given me the drink came over and said, "You've just won me a pound note, Doc," he said, "and I'm grateful to you."

"How's that?" I asked.

"Johnny Joe over there," and he nodded towards his grinning friend, "said you'd all the mackerel out of you and I said there was more to come so we put a bet on it."

"I'm glad to be of help," I said ruefully.

Big Jim was having no problem with his stomach, in fact quite the opposite. When I began to feel a little better, I went down to the galley to make a cup of tea. Jim was sitting at the table, knife and fork already in his hands about to start into an enormous fry up.

"Are you crazy, Jim?" I said as I looked at his plate piled high with bacon, sausages, fried soda bread and three eggs all covered in beans and tomato sauce. "You'll send your blood sugar through the roof with that lot inside you."

"It's O.K. Doc, don't you worry yourself, I've everything under control. I'm stabilising the diabetes now. I brought the sugar down with the whiskey, now I'm putting it back up with a little food"

There was no point in arguing with him. I made a cup of tea.

"Is there one in the pot for me?" he asked between mouthfuls.

"There is," I told him and poured him one. "Do you take milk?"

"Aye, a drop of milk would be grand and a drop of sugar too while you're at it."

"Sugar," I exclaimed, "in your tea and you a diabetic. I don't think that's a good idea."

"It's all part of the stabilising exercise, Doc," Jim said with a grin.

"How many sugars then?" I asked.

"Six."

"Six. But that's crazy, Jim. Do you want to kill yourself altogether?"

"I'm cutting back," he said.

"Cutting back? What do you mean, cutting back?"

"I used to take twelve but they started to rot my teeth so I had to cut it back to six."

"You're too hard on yourself, Jim," I said sarcastically. "Couldn't you have tried eight or nine first? You know, break yourself in gradually"

"No, no, Doc, I had to be drastic. I had to save the teeth. There was nothing else for it but cut it right down to six."

I gave up. I drank my tea in silence and began to feel a little better. I went back on deck to see what was going on. The crew were hauling in the nets and were excited about something. A small shark was caught and they were afraid to untangle it from the net in case they were bitten. In the end, they cut a large section out and threw it into the sea. We watched as the shark wriggled and freed itself and swam off. It was a lovely sight seeing such a powerful fish swim like a shadow beneath the moonlit surface of the sea. The fishermen weren't as pleased though as they thought of the loss of their net.

There were salmon being pulled in by the dozen. Some of them had been half eaten by dog fish. They were also caught in the nets but that didn't seem to please the fishermen either as they threw them back into the sea after clubbing them on the head. The excitement died down when the nets had been emptied and the fish stowed away.

We headed back to port. The fishermen went down to their berths for a lie down. Big Jim and I stood on the deck searching for the first glimpse of land. The sun was starting to come up over the mountains when we saw the hazy outline of the Kerry coastline. The mountain ridges were bathed in a golden light and cast their long shadows down the dark gulleys towards the sea. Smoke drifted lazily from the chimneys of white cottages perched high in the hills. A soft sea mist shrouded the lower valleys but, even as we watched, we could see it beginning to lift and reveal a wakening world.

Big Jim was deeply affected by the beauty of it all. "Did you ever, in all of your living life, see the likes of that James?" he said, his voice choking with emotion. Before I could reply, he continued, "When God made the world all those thousands of years ago, do you know what He said?"

"No, Jim. I wasn't around then."

There was a moment's silence.

"I know you weren't around then, James but somebody must have been because my teacher at the National School knew what He said and she told me."

I could see his story was going to take a long time so I played along with him.

"Well then, what did He say?"

"I'm going to tell you what He said if you'd only be a little patient. Do you know something James, you can be a very impatient young man sometimes for someone so young as yourself. That's not good for you. It puts the blood pressure up and that's not good for anybody in the long run."

"OK, OK ,Jim" I said looking up to heaven. "I'll try to be more patient in future. Now, can you tell me what God said about the creation of Kerry?"

"Am I not coming to that?" Big Jim said. "And there you go again with that impatience of yours. I'll tell you now what He said if you'd only give me the time. He said and if anyone should know what He's talking about, He does."

"Who does, Jim?"

"God does. Are you listening to me at all? Did they not teach you nothing about God creating the world at school?"

Before I could answer, he had started up again.

"God said 'I will create a beautiful Emerald Isle and call it Ireland. It will be the jewel in my earthly crown. No island or land in all the world will compare with it's unsurpassable beauty. And in that island I will put the Kingdom of Kerry, the gem of all Ireland, the most magnificent of all my creations.'"

Jim looked at me very solemnly.

"And do you know why He said that?"

"I think he maybe had the Kerry tourist board in mind, Jim" I couldn't resist saying.

"Are you daft altogether, James? There was no tourist boards about in them days. He said it because He wanted everybody to know there is nothing in the world to compare with the sun rising over the Kerry Mountains. It's incomparable. Isn't that what I've been trying to tell you, if only you had the patience to listen. And that's why He said it."

I didn't know if Big Jim was being serious or not but as I gazed at the beauty of the approaching land bathed in the early morning sunlight, I almost began to believe him.

Meningitis

That magical trip with Big Jim, Phil Ban and the boat crew out on the high seas buoyed my spirits up for days. It was just as well because it gave me the energy and strength to deal with one of the most frightening and serious conditions a doctor can ever encounter – meningitis. Meningitis is a word that strikes fear into the hearts of everyone, both parents and doctors alike.

I remember when I was twelve, my sister, Maria, who was then three years old, got up as happy as could be one morning. By lunchtime she had developed a slight temperature and by four o'clock, she had fallen into a coma.

My parents were extremely alarmed and rushed her to the children's fever hospital. By the time they arrived there, she was unconscious and breathing in deep snorts. The junior doctor called a consultant to see her immediately.

The consultant, Dr Finlay, took one look at Maria and said she needed a lumbar puncture (LP) at once. A lumbar puncture is a procedure where a long needle is introduced into the lower back to draw off fluid around the spinal cord (cerebro-spinal fluid – CSF) – usually to find out if a patient has meningitis.

On rare occasions the procedure can be hazardous, something my parents were only too aware of. It can be particularly dangerous if the pressure of the cerebral spinal fluid is raised before the LP is done. In such situations a LP can cause a rapid loss of CSF which makes the lower part of the brain fall on to the base of the skull – a condition called coning.

When the brain cones, the breathing centre at the bottom of the brain becomes trapped and the patient stops breathing. Death usually follows rapidly. At the same time, if a definite diagnosis of meningitis is to be made, a lumbar puncture is essential despite the risk. The risk of not diagnosing meningitis correctly is much greater than the risk of coning.

My parents were asked to wait outside while Dr Finlay did the LP. He came out ten minutes later looking very sombre. "I'm very sorry to have to tell you Paddy and you too Joan that your little girl is very ill. Very, very ill. She is in a very bad way, a very, very bad way indeed. I hate to have to say this to you and I'm truly sorry for having to be so blunt but in all honesty, I can't see Maria surviving the night. I feel in the circumstances, I have to prepare you for the worst."

My mother burst out crying. She cried and cried and just couldn't stop herself. My father put his arm round her shoulders as he tried to console her. She told me later that when Dr Finlay told them Maria was critically ill and not likely to survive, everything in the room seemed to stand still.

"All I could think of was that he had said my lovely little girl, the light of my life - Maria was going to die. I couldn't take it in. I just couldn't believe him. I stared at Dr Finlay in complete disbelief. His lips went on moving and I knew he was saying something but I couldn't hear him. I could hear nothing. The room was in a haze. Everything seemed a long, long way away and then objects suddenly started rushing at me. I felt dizzy and thought I was going to pass out. I vaguely remember your father and Dr Finlay half carrying me to our car.

We were not allowed to stay with Maria that night. Nobody was allowed to stay with their sick child in those days no matter how ill they were or who the parents were. It was the rule of the time and we just accepted it. I could only think the next time I saw my little girl, she would be lying in her little white coffin.

I don't remember the journey home. It was all a blur like you see on films when someone gets a knock on the head and everything around them seems as if it is in a dream. Your father told me later I talked and acted like a robot. Fortunately he kept his cool even though his heart must have been breaking at the thought of losing his Daddy's little girl.

He told me later that when Dr Finlay did the lumbar puncture, instead of getting crystal clear liquid which is what normal CSF looks like, he found thick green pus oozing out of the end of the lumbar puncture needle, a sign of an overwhelming infection and almost a sure sign of death."

"To tell you the truth, Paddy, and I hate to have to tell you but I feel you have to know to prepare yourself for the worst," Dr Finlay had said to my father privately, once they had helped my mother into the car, "I've never seen CSF as bad as that before in my entire life and I've been doing lumbar punctures for thirty years."

"If by some miracle Maria does survive," Dr Finlay continued, "its very likely she will be brain damaged, deaf or blind, possibly all three. You saw yourself how quickly the meningococcal rash spread over her skin in the time it took you to drive here. I don't have to tell you, you know yourselves what can happen when children of this age get a bad Meningococcal septicaemia."

My father nodded his head. He knew only too well. He didn't want to hear any more.

I remember my parents coming home that day without Maria. It is etched in my memory. We wanted to know where she was and why they had left her behind and why my mother was crying so much. It made us all cry to see her so upset.

"Maria's very sick, very, very sick," my father told us, his voice choking, "it looks as though she's going to die. That's why your mother's crying."

"Maria's not going to die, Daddy," we cried. "Maria can't die and leave us all." Maria was the youngest in the family and everybody loved her.

"There's nothing we can do to stop it," he said. "Maria is just very, very ill and there's nothing I can do to help her."

He wanted us to be prepared for the worst.

Dr Finlay had given her less than one in a hundred chance of living through the night. The brown purple rash had spread rapidly through her body and large areas of her skin were covered in coalescing blotches, usually the sign of a hopeless prognosis. We were all crying and that made my father, who had been holding back his tears with difficulty, cry too. It was the first time in my life I'd ever seen him crying and that alarmed me. He was always so strong and upbeat, afraid of nothing. If my father was crying and could do nothing, then things had to be bad, very, very bad indeed.

I remember the next four days better than any other days of my life. They are imprinted on my memory as though struck there with a brandishing iron. For the first time in my short life, I knew what worry was. I was so worried I could hardly eat and had difficulty sleeping. I tossed and turned all night.

My father insisted life go on as normally as possible. I was sent to my piano lesson that evening. I remember staring blankly at the sheets of music and seeing nothing. All I could think of was that by the time I got home, Maria would be dead. My music teacher was a gentle old lady who had been brought up in the Victorian era. She got very miffed with me and thumped the piano keys when I made no response. She hadn't heard about Maria. The music score which generally looked like Greek to me now looked like a text of Egyptian hieroglyphics.

When my father phoned the hospital the following morning, Maria was still alive but in a deep coma. She had stopped passing urine and had gone into kidney failure on top of everything else.

My parents were very religious. They got us to pray and pray until our knees ached. My mother had a sister called Eileen who had just returned from a trip to Italy. When she had been in Italy, she had visited a holy Friar called Padre Pio who lived in the monastery of San Giovanni Rotondo in the district of Foggia.

She said seeing that holy man was the most extraordinary and unbelievable experience of her life. Neither she nor her husband had ever met anyone remotely like him before. She told my mother that even though she was twenty yards away from Padre Pio and in the middle of a thronging crowd who were trying to get close to him, she felt there something extraordinary about the man.

"I could feel an incredible aura of goodness emanating from him. I felt as if I was being given some sort of an inkling of what it will be like to meet God face to face. It was an unbelievably wonderful experience. We must all pray to Padre Pio and ask him to ask God to intercede for Maria and make her better," she said. "I have no doubt whatsoever he will help her." Eileen was a woman of deep simple faith. It was just what we needed at a time like that.

Even though my mother was religious, she was sceptical about believing in a man like that unless she had actually seen him herself. Nevertheless, she got us all to kneel down and pray to Padre Pio to ask God and his Holy Mother to cure Maria.

My mother told me some time later that almost immediately after our prayers, she felt a tremendous sense of calm. She just somehow knew there and then that everything was going to be alright and that Maria was going to get better. She stopped worrying, to my father's amazement, and after that she kept all our spirits up.

Maria remained in a coma for four days. On the afternoon of the fourth day during their half hour visit, my parents noticed Maria was breathing normally and the horrible snorting respiration that had alarmed them so much had settled. When they were about to leave, Maria opened her eyes.

"Mammy, Daddy," she whispered and closed her eyes again.

My father said it was the happiest moment of his life. He ran out to find a phone to call home. We all jumped and shouted for joy and, when my parents came home an hour later we were given the biggest bottles of lemonade and as many biscuits and sweets as we could eat.

Maria made a complete recovery though it was very slow. She stayed in hospital for a month and when she came home, she was emaciated. Her growth stopped for nearly two years while she recovered her strength. Because she was so weak, she was unable to start school at the proper time and had to delay it a year. Her appetite was poor.

We had a woman called Brigid at the time, who helped my mother out. She cleaned and tidied the house and cooked some of our meals. Brigid was shocked that, despite having two doctors in the house, nobody had thought about giving Maria a tonic. She went on so much about the tonic that, in the end, my father got Maria one to get some peace from Brigid. Maria refused to take it so he entrusted the administration of it to Brigid.

Brigid was only too willing and, from then on, Maria had her tonic twice a day, whether she wanted it or not or whether it helped her or not. Brigid attributed Marias cure to the tonic. After that,7 Ballatines, the local chemist, couldn't stock enough of it.

Everybody walked to school in the 1960s but Maria wasn't fit enough to walk even a short distance. My mother had to get her old black and yellow pram down from the attic and dust it down so Maria could ride in it to and from school. She was happy to sit in it and be pushed. We used to tease her about being the only primary one pupil in the whole of Ireland who was pushed to school in a pram.

Despite Dr Finlay's prognosis, the meningitis left Maria with no long term effects. She qualified in medicine twenty years later and said the time in hospital with the doctors and nurses was what made her want to study medicine, though I think my father advising her to become a doctor at least once a week might have had something to do with it as well.

My Aunt Eileen put Maria's recovery down to prayer and Padre Pio and repeated endlessly, "More things are wrought by prayer than this world dreams of."

Two years later, my father went on a pilgrimage of Thanksgiving to San Giovanni Rotondo where Padre Pio lived. He talked about it for a long time afterwards. As Padre Pio passed through the crowds, he caught my father's eye and raised his eyebrows as if in recognition. He smiled as he said one word, "Maria?" and moved on.

When I was a medical student and a junior doctor, I never saw a single case of meningitis. Despite the enormous fear the disease causes, it is fortunately quite a rare condition. One G.P. I know never saw a single case of meningitis in his whole medical career. I wasn't so fortunate.

I had been working in Slievegart two months when I was called out one night at midnight by a man who was worried about his son. He sounded anxious. Usually phone calls about a sick child, are made by the wife or mother of the family. When the wife gets her husband to make the call it usually means she thinks there is something seriously wrong, especially where a child is concerned.

"Hello Doctor. This is Mr Tracey of Hannasford. I'm really worried about my son, Kevin. He's fourteen and since he came home from playing football this evening, he's been behaving strangely."

"In what way strangely?" I asked. I didn't like the sound of that. It was before the time of drugs and drinking in teenagers.

"Well, one minute he knows where he is and the next he's talking complete gibberish. A couple of minutes ago he started having a chat with his Granny but she's been dead for the last two years. We tried to make him understand but he's insisting that he can see her."

"Did he get a knock on his head during the game?" I asked "Has he a temperature?"

I wanted to rule out Kevin being delirious. A high temperature is a common cause for confusion but more so in children under ten.

"He feels a bit warm but nothing special," the father replied.

"Do you see any dark spots on his skin?"

This was before all the scares about meningitis and all the information leaflets and public awareness about the infection. Most people in those days wouldn't have given a thought or known anything about the meningococcal rash.

"No, I don't see anything different in his skin, do you Eleanor?" he said asking his wife.

"Well Michael, I was just wondering about that little black spot on his arm there. I hadn't noticed it before."

"Would it mean anything if it was new?" I heard her asking.

I had heard enough. I asked directions to their house and ran to the Landrover. I drove as fast as I could. If my suspicions were right, Kevin was already seriously ill with meningitis. The family lived seven miles away at the foot of the Kerry Mountains on the coast road. Mr Tracey was waiting for me at the end of his laneway looking extremely anxious. He must have heard the anxiety in my voice.

Diagnosing and treating a case of meningitis outside the safe confines of a hospital had me extremely worried too. When you see the purple/brown spots and they are due to meningococal bacteria, it means the patient has meningococcal septicaemia (blood poisoning) at the very least. Septicaemia can occur on its own but is usually accompanied by meningitis. In Kevin's case, it looked as though he had both infections, the septicaemia and the meningitis.

I screeched the Landrover to a halt outside their cottage, I grabbed my bag and ran inside. I shouted to the father to phone for an ambulance to come immediately. Mrs Tracey showed me into the sitting room where Kevin was tossing and turning restlessly on the sofa. He looked completely dazed.

"Since you called, I've been watching Kevin's skin," his mother said, "and a few more of those black spots have come out. What does that mean doctor?"

"Where are they?" I demanded. I didn't have time to explain and, in any case, I didn't want to alarm her even more about my suspicions.

She pointed to seven or eight brown spots scattered over his stomach and arms. I pressed my finger against them. They didn't disappear.

"How are you feeling, Kevin?" I asked as I hastily opened my bag to take out a vial of penicillin.

"Who are you?" he asked, staring at me with wide-open eyes. "Are you the man that fixes motor boat engines because if you are, you're a bit late."

"No, not exactly, Kevin," I said. "I'm not that man. I'm the doctor and I'm going to have to give you a little injection into your arm if you don't mind to help settle you down a bit."

"No, no, no," he started screaming. "You're not going to give me any injections. I'm not having any injections. I don't need settling down. There's nothing wrong with me. Go away, go away."

He began to throw himself around on the sofa like a wildcat lashing out with his hands and feet in all directions.

His mother looked at me and then at Kevin in complete alarm.

"Doctor," she said, "that's not our Kevin. That's not our Kevin at all. He's not like that. He's never rude and he is not afraid of injections. He must be putting this all on, some sort of silly practical joke. He's never been bothered about injections in the past. He just laughs at them and treats them like a joke"

"He's not putting it on, Mrs Tracey. It's the illness he has that's making him behave like that."

"What do you mean, the illness he has? Why? What sort of illness do you think he has? What do you think is wrong with him?" She was now thoroughly alarmed. Her husband had come back into the room and he looked as anxious as his wife. I was feeling extremely anxious myself and trying my best to hide it. I felt away out of my depth having to deal with a serious case of meningitis on my own in a small cottage in the middle of nowhere.

"Look, please. If you don't mind, I'll explain in a minute. I've got to get this injection into Kevin first." The urgency and tremor in my voice put them into even more of a panic.

Meningitis can sometimes spread with alarming speed and catastrophic results. As soon as it is suspected, penicillin must be given intravenously immediately. If a patient is allergic to penicillin another antibiotic must be used like Erythromycin.

"Can you hold his arm steady, Mr Tracey while I draw up the penicillin? He's not allergic to penicillin is he?"

"No, he's not allergic to anything," his father said as he tried to catch hold of his son's flailing arms.

Kevin fought like an alley cat. He was determined he wasn't going to have any injection, meningitis or no meningitis.

"What on earth are you playing at, Kevin?" his father shouted. He was getting cross but his annoyance was tempered with anxiety.

"Just hold his arm steady, Michael, no matter what it takes, just hold his arms," Mrs Tracey cried out.

Michael slipped behind his son and took hold of him in a full Nelson hold which allowed Mrs Tracey to straighten out his right arm. Kevin was kicking out with his legs like someone crazy as he tried to break free. His mother was screaming and sobbing at the same time.

"What's wrong with you Kevin? Why are you doing this? Why are you behaving like this? Oh, Doctor, there must be something terribly wrong with him. He's never behaved like this before in his life. He's normally such a nice quiet, boy. This isn't him at all"

She was so agitated she wasn't holding Kevin's arm steady enough for me to give the penicillin injection. There was no way I could give an intravenous injection into a crooked moving target the way Kevin was flinging his arms about.

"You've got to hold his arm steady or I'll not be able to put the needle into his vein, Mrs Tracey," I shouted. "I'll sit on his legs to stop him kicking. You must keep his arm still for twenty seconds until I've given him the penicillin"

It took a lot of strength to hold his arm straight but in the end she managed to do it. I found the soft part of his elbow. He had good veins and I was able to give him the injection he needed so badly. We all stepped away and Kevin fell back on to the sofa completely exhausted.

Thirty seconds later, he suddenly sat bolt upright and looked at me with surprise.

"Hello Doctor, what are you doing here?" he asked. "I wasn't expecting to see you."

I was amazed by his immediate response to the penicillin. It was too good to be true. Kevin talked normally to his parents for about a minute and then, suddenly, collapsed into unconsciousness. He stopped breathing for ten seconds which seemed to me to go on forever. I thought my injection had killed him. I was completely panic stricken and thumped his chest in desperation. To my enormous relief, he started breathing again, though his breaths came in snorts that terrified his parents and me.

Mrs Tracey put her hands over her mouth and screamed.

"Oh no, no, no. He's dying. Our Kevin's dying. What are we going to do? Oh Michael, what are we going to do?"

I didn't know what was happening. Apart from everything else, I was concerned Kevin was allergic to penicillin after all and my injection had finished him off.

Kevin's grunting breathing settled down after what seemed an eternity. Seeing someone breathe like that is extremely frightening to anybody who has ever witnessed it, especially if you think you may have caused it.

"Where is that ambulance," I kept asking myself.

Mrs Tracey was on the verge of becoming hysterical. I knew what I was about to ask her was going to make her worse but I had to do it.

"Do you have any other children, Mrs Tracey?"

I was right. My question made her worse, a lot worse.

"Yes, two. Why? Why are you asking? Are they going to have the same thing as Kevin?" and she started to sob uncontrollably.

Mr Tracey had made himself a space on the sofa beside Kevin and was holding his hand. He was doing his best to remain calm.

"Look, Mrs Tracey, I know it's extremely difficult but you've got to settle yourself down for a few minutes for Kevin's sake," I told her. "I need to have a look at your two other children to make sure they're alright.

She made an effort to control her tears as she ran out of the room returning thirty seconds later with two sleepy boys of eight and twelve. I asked them how they felt. They both said they felt fine. I looked at the skin of the eight year old first and it was clear. When I checked the torso of the older boy, I was astounded to find he was covered in a meningocoal rash. The rash seemed to have spread over 30% of his body.

"Are you sure you feel alright, Tommy?" I asked. "You haven't got a head ache or feel a bit shivery?"

"No, I'm O.K." Charlie replied. "I just feel a bit tired."

"You don't feel like vomiting?"

Tommy shook his head. He insisted he felt OK.

When his mother saw the rash on his stomach, she was beside herself with anxiety. I hadn't mentioned the possibility of meningitis yet but she knew something was seriously wrong. You can be the best actor in the world but there aren't many doctors that can completely disguise their feelings in situations like that. I certainly couldn't anyway, at that stage in my career.

I checked Tommy over carefully but, apart from the rash, I couldn't find anything else wrong with him. I gave him a shot of penicillin to be on the safe side. When the ambulance arrived a half hour later after one of the thirty most anxious minutes of my life, I sent the whole family to the Accident and Emergency Department to be checked out. Kevin was still unconscious. As they carried him out, I noticed his two feet had almost turned black. I followed the ambulance to Tralee hospital in case he deteriorated on the way.

The A and E Department admitted Kevin and Tommy to their intensive care unit immediately. When I phoned the next day, Kevin was still unconscious. Despite Tommy's extensive rash, he was perfectly fit and was discharged two days later. The rest of the family had no signs of infection.

Kevin was lucky to survive. He had a stormy recovery. By the time he was admitted to hospital he was deeply unconscious and his back was arching to an alarming degree (opisthotonos).

His feet had turned completely black. He remained in a coma for two days and only came out of it gradually.

The consultant in charge of intensive care initially thought he would have to amputate both of Kevin's feet to stop gangrene spreading throughout his body. In the end Kevin lost three toes from his right foot and two from his left.

He stayed in hospital for six weeks and when he came out, he was only skin and bone. His parents were extremely thankful for my rapid intervention and sang my praises around Slievegart. They presented me with an enormous salmon a week later that kept myself and the two cats in the finest fettle for several days.

I didn't see another case of meningitis for several years and when I did it was an epidemic in the middle of a West African jungle.

Jaws

When I was a medical student, I thought I would like to be a children's doctor when I qualified. I enjoyed the innocence of children and their sense of fun. They made me laugh and I loved the way they talked and the funny things they said. I changed my mind though during my houseman's year.

There was a busy Accident and Emergency department at the Dublin Hospital where I was working. Part of my duties was to help out in the casualty department.

One Saturday evening, a ten year old girl was brought in by ambulance. She had been knocked off her bicycle by a drunk driver. Her skull was fractured and she died shortly after being admitted. I was there when she died and I was there two hours later when her distraught father came in to identify her. I had to take him to the morgue and it was one of the most distressing things I ever had to do in my medical career. He sobbed uncontrollably when he saw his dead daughter's frail little body with her head swathed in white bandages lying on the cold mortuary slab.

"My little girl, my little girl," he cried out. "That isn't her. That can't be my little girl. Please tell me that isn't her," and he caught hold of my sleeve and cried and cried.

I felt numb for a week. I cannot even begin to imagine how the poor father felt.

My interest in Paediatrics took a bad knock after that. I thought I wouldn't be too good at handling children dying and their parents' grief.

Two weeks after that accident, the department was put on red alert. There had been a major traffic accident not far from the hospital. Five people had been killed and many others injured. I rushed to the A and E department and met up with the doctors and nurses waiting for the casualties to arrive. Two ambulances screeched to a halt and we all rushed out to open the doors. We needed to assess the degree of injuries quickly and deal with the most severe cases. I pulled the door open of the first ambulance. It contained the bodies of a boy of five and a little girl of three. The parents were sitting beside their dead children and they were in a state of complete shock. Blood was streaming from their heads but they didn't seem to notice. They sat there, staring aghast at their dead children. Several of the nurses began to cry and two of the doctors turned away. I was completely unprepared for anything like this.

That scene remained etched on my mind for years. The second ambulance brought in their third child, a girl of twelve who was seriously injured. It turned out later her spinal cord had been severed. She would never walk again. What was especially poignant to me was that she was the same age as my sister Maria and was wearing a similar lilac coloured dress that Maria liked to wear on special occasions.

I know that doctors are supposed to always be professional and put things like that behind them and get on with their work and normally we do but sometimes the memories of events like that haunt you for years and sometimes for the rest of your life.

Despite those two traumatic experiences, I still enjoyed working with children. During my time at Slievegart, when I opened the surgery door I was always delighted to find the waiting room full of two, three or four year olds waiting to see me except of course if they had come for their vaccinations when sometimes the morning would develop into an awful howling match.

The children of that era were almost without exception, extremely well behaved. That was long before the famous children's gurus notion of 'express yourself at all times and repress nothing' mentality became popular.

When I called a family into the surgery, the children always waited for their mother to go in first and then they would follow. The chair was always for mother and not for the first scrambling child to get to it. The children would stand quietly to one side of her as she sat down. The child who was unwell was lifted onto the mother's knee for me to examine. The other children would look on with great interest. They never spoke or made a sound.

Sweets were a treat in those days. I made myself popular with the Slievegart children, but not with their school dentist, by giving them all a penny chew at the end of the consultation and there was always a subdued thank you.

I only came across one badly behaved child in my whole time in Slievegart. His behaviour had more to do with his parents' lack of common sense and their idea of being ahead of their time with their opinions and thinking. They had spent three years in America doing post graduate studies and had read every word the children's gurus had ever written. They took the gurus' work as gospel and were determined that their little Zachary wasn't going to be backward about coming forward like they regarded generations of other repressed Irish children to have been.

I knew as soon as I opened the waiting room door that day, that two year old Zak had what the Americans now call a serious 'attitood' problem. He was sitting in the middle of the floor holding court. He wasn't exactly very fat but he was a big boy with a red sweating face squeezed into a sailor suit with buttons that were so stretched they were unable to hold the material together.

The other children in the room were tucked in beside their mothers watching Zak's extraordinary antics with mesmerised fascination. Zak's parents, Bill and Jane were looking at Zak too but with an admiration and chest bursting love that bordered on the pathological.

Zak had got hold of one of the waiting room magazines and was shredding it methodically into tiny pieces with a steely determination which I almost had to admire. His parents cooingly praised his every effort. The other mothers were horrified that these two, who were only visitors to the village, were allowing Zak to destroy Doctor Robert's property. One of them, Mrs Doyle, the mother of ten children remonstrated with Zak's parents but Bill was having none of that.

"Hey lady, now you listen to me," I heard him say through the half open surgery door, "this doctor guy left these magazines in reach of my little kid. That means where I'm coming from and where all the progressive thinkers are coming from that they are there for kids to use. If he didn't want kids to use them, then he should've put them out of their reach. Do you think my Zak wants to read about some third hand automobile that's for sale in a ten year old rubbishy magazine. No way, lady. So what does he do. He tears them rubbishy magazines up. That's a statement Zak's making. That's called self-expression. That's Zak's way of letting that doctor know he doesn't feel too good about him leaving out rubbish magazines to entertain little guys of his age. Where are the kids' toys for me to play with, that's what Zak's asking. Zak wants this guy Roberts to move out of the dark ages and start listening to little guys like him. We can all learn from guys like Zak." Even through the half opened door, I could sense Mrs Doyle's boiling anger as Bill continued. "You have a choice to make here yourself, lady. You can try and learn something from Zak about self expression and being a free thinker or you can take a hike back into the past and take your repressed kids with you."

I had listened to all this with increasing amazement.

I rushed to call Mrs Doyle in before open war broke out in the waiting room. The normally placid Mrs Doyle was red in the face and looking extremely cross, so cross in fact, I was afraid she might rush across the waiting room and hit Bill with her handbag. I hastily invited her to sit down. She had five of her children with her. They followed her in quietly, a bit different to Zak who was screaming with rage because Mrs Doyle had put the rest of the magazines out of his reach.

Mrs Doyle sat down. Her nostrils were flaring and her normally gentle eyes seemed to be bulging. She had difficulty finding her words and didn't speak for several seconds. She eventually managed to gasp, "I'm really sorry, Dr Griffin for behaving like this especially as I'm only here to get treatment for Brendan's ringworm to stop it spreading round the family but, in all your life, did you ever see such a child as that spoilt brat Zak and as stupid a man as his father.

I've never heard anyone in all my life, whether they be rich or poor, sane or insane, talk such nonsense. If that's what book learning and studying and letters after your name does for you, we'd all be better off staying ignorant. What's he doing here at this time of the day, anyway? Shouldn't he be out with the fishing or making hay or at his work or out walking the dog instead of fussing over that child of his? He should leave the mothering of the child to his wife.

Mrs Doyle held the strong conventional views of the time. Certain tasks were men's work and others were strictly women's. In Mrs Doyle's eyes, bringing a child to the surgery was women's work.

"I'm in a tricky situation here," I thought. I didn't want to criticise Bill or Zak because that would soon have gotten round the town but, at the same time, I would have to let Mrs Doyle feel I was sympathetic to her view point without actually saying so. I needed to keep Mrs Doyle happy and get her blood pressure to come down as well.

"Yes indeed, Mrs Doyle," I said, "the world is moving on at a terrific pace, too fast for a lot of us. There are so many changes taking place and not all of them for the better. Evidently a child's ability to express itself is considered important in America, other countries too. It takes all sorts doesn't it in this changing world.

Mrs Doyle snorted. She was having none of it. "Self expression, my foot," she said. "Where would we be if we all went round expressing ourselves every time we felt like it like that whippersnapper Zak and his fool of a father? If we did, my husband would have his dinner over his head instead of in his stomach more times than enough. You mark my words, Dr Griffin, if that self expression nonsense from America or wherever it comes from gets a grip across the rest of the world, then, in ten or twenty years time, everything will be upside down.

There'll be no more religion or marriage or responsibility or law and order or consideration for anybody. You'll have gangs of lads like that there Zak and his stupid father going round expressing themselves, satisfying themselves, denying themselves nothing whenever and wherever they feel like it. What sort of society will that lead to if everybody is a greedy, self expressing, self centered, good for nothing?"

I could see Mrs Doyle was just warming up and I would have the benefit of her opinion for the next half an hour or so if I let her carry on.

"You could have a valid point there, Mrs Doyle," I said trying to placate her. "There could be big changes ahead if things keep going the way they are. Talking of trouble, Brendan here has a right dose of ringworm on his head, Mrs Doyle, I'll have to give you a big tube of cream to put on his scalp three times a day for the next six weeks. And by the way, how is your husband? What did he think of Kerry giving Cork a hammering last week? That must have pleased him."

Mrs Doyle smiled for the first time. Her husband came from Cork and he was a fanatical Gaelic football supporter of the Cork team. Mrs Doyle herself was a Kerry supporter. When Cork played Kerry, the Doyle household went into mourning for a week no matter which side won. One of the couple was sure to be a loser and whichever one it was went around the house as if someone had died. The children knew better than to support either side.

I showed the now smiling Mrs Doyle to the door. She gave Bill an icy look as she passed. He didn't seem to notice at first and then he sat up and shouted after her, "Hey, take care lady, remember what I said. Loosen up a bit and find yourself and the kids some freedom. Get yourself a life."

Mrs Doyle stalked out of the room, with the children marching behind her, muttering about spoilt children with idiotic parents.

I sighed with relief that things hadn't developed any further between them. I knew that the usually gentle Mrs Doyle, when she got fired up, would be quite capable of clobbering Bill. Bill certainly seemed to merit an award as one of the most insensitive, totally self-centred men I had ever seen and I hadn't even spoken to him yet.

I called them into my office. Zak was in the middle of a particularly difficult bit of magazine shredding and didn't like being disturbed. Bill had no notion of disturbing him either.

"Hi Doc, hold on a minute will ya? The little guy has nearly finished."

I looked at the red faced, fat boy squatting on the middle of the floor surrounded by heaps of torn paper. His little jowels were sucking furiously on a huge blue comforter as he tried to tear the last of Dr Robert's ancient magazine to pieces.

At last, Zak finished and Bill encouraged the little man to his feet. Zak gave a couple of angry snorts and sucking more violently on his comforter, tried to shove his father away. Bill lifted the protesting child up gently and, marching into the surgery, sat the roaring Zak down on a chair. He knelt beside him as if in homage.

"There, there, little lad, I'm sorry I had to pick you up like that my little Zakky Wakky. I know you don't like it but we must have you checked out by this guy here. He's what's called a doctor," Bill started to explain to the squirming Zak.

Then he went on to explain who a doctor was and what he did and how he worked, pronouncing all his words with a strong American accent. Zak was still screaming in protest like a bear who had caught its foot in a snare at having been lifted before he was good and ready. I wondered how this man who came from Castlebar had managed to pick up such a corny accent when he had only lived in the United States for three years.

"Well now," I began. I knew if I didn't get started, Bill would be happy to carry on with his lengthy explanations for the next half hour.

He didn't take any notice.

"Well now," I repeated some six decibels higher, "exactly what is wrong with Zak?"

Bill turned his head to look at me. He had a sly 'I've caught you out' look on his face.

"That's why we're here, Jimmy," he said. "We want you to tell us what's wrong with Zak. You're the doc aren't you?"

I immediately felt the hackles on the back of my neck begin to rise. I disliked being called Jimmy especially by someone I had never met before in my life. I also didn't like the smart Alec remark of the variety that tells me what my job is. Bill was oblivious to my sudden mood change and I don't expect he would have cared if he had noticed. He blundered on.

"You guys sure have it easy, seeing a few kids in your office and then heading home to count all the big bucks you've been earning for doing next to nothing."

I could see straight away that Bill and I were never going to make it as friends. I decided I was not going to argue with him but just try to get him out of my office as soon as possible.

"When you say Zak is feeling unwell, do you mean to say he has a high temperature or has he been vomiting or coughing?"

"No, I didn't say anything about any of that. Nobody said anything about Zak feeling unwell or mentioned vomiting or coughing." He turned to his wife. "Did you hear me say anything about vomiting or coughing? Did you see my lips move?"

Bill guffawed at his own special brand of humour as I wondered to myself, "What sort of a clown is this?"

"Only kidding you, Jimmy," he said and leaning forward, he punched me twice on the shoulder, boom, boom. "Got ya there, Jimmy boy."

I am normally a reasonably calm, non-confrontational type of person but Bill was beginning to get under my skin. I gritted my teeth and tightened the grip on my pen.

"Thank you for sharing that humour with me Mr O'Keefe but could we just move on to what is Zak's problem?" I asked coldly.

"Hey, what's with the Mr O'Keefe, Jimmy. Call me Bill, in fact you can call me anything but don't call me too early in the morning. Boom. Boom," and Bill laughed long and loud at his own joke.

I remember thinking I would have to remember that 'Boom, boom'. I reckoned it must have been some sort of trade mark for the man's humour, his way of alerting himself and others to the fact that he had just been funny again.

"Mr O'Keefe, I would like to move on with this interview if you don't mind and get Zak sorted out. I have other patients waiting to be seen"

My words didn't have any effect on him at all. His skin was as thick as a rhinoceros. He went on cooing and tickling Zak. Nobody was going to rush him or his Zak. As far as he was concerned, if I was under pressure to see other patients, that was my problem.

I turned to his wife.

"Mrs O'Keefe, could you please tell me what your concerns are about Zak?" I asked.

Mrs O'Keefe was a timid, mousey little woman in her early thirties who didn't seem to have too many opinions of her own. She immediately turned to look at her husband as though seeking his approval before she spoke. Bill frowned. "Is somebody overlooking me?" He seemed to be thinking. He obviously didn't like missing out on anything, no matter how trivial it might be.

"Hey, Jimmy, I'm running this show," he said petulantly. "I'm the guy that's been looking after Zak's health needs for the last two weeks. Jane's been...."

"O.K. then," I interrupted Bill's monologue. "How's Zak been?"

I worded my sentence carefully. I didn't want to leave an opening for another of his humour strikes. Boom, boom.

"The little guy's been up and down. He's off his food," Bill said in a huffy voice. He wasn't used to being interrupted.

I looked down at Zak's chubby cheeks chomping down like a piston on to his soother. Maybe being off his food for a day or two wasn't such a bad thing for the little man.

"No vomiting, no diarrhoea or cough?" I asked.

"Nah, none of that stuff," Bill said, "Just off form. The little guy needs checking out, a physical, that's all."

It was all a bit vague but there was something I could lock onto. Give Zak a physical, check him out. I would examine him, give him the all clear and Boom, boom, I would have Bill, his free spirit and his family out of my office.

"O.K.," I said, "let's have a look at Zak." I leant forward slightly to look at his skin to see if there were any spots. Zak wasn't on for having anyone looking at him let alone touch him. He immediately turned round and squirmed up his father's chest and halfway over his shoulder like a baboon clambering up a tree. I was surprised at his turn of speed especially for such a fat child.

Bill caught hold of him and shouted at me angrily, "Hey, Jimmy boy, what's up with you? You nearly scared the life out of the little guy and made him fall off my shoulder. You ought to introduce yourself to Zak, have a chat with him first before you start poking about and examining him."

Bill seemed to like giving these little lectures. He felt it put him in control. He was right though about getting a child to relax before examining it but I wasn't going to admit that to him. When you are dealing with a spoilt child, you do have to take much more time approaching and pandering to them but that was not the norm in those days. I had already wasted twenty minutes of my time with Bill and Zak and had got nowhere. I had reached the stage where I just wanted them out of the surgery and out of my hair – forever.

"Sorry Bill," I said. I was prepared to say almost anything to get things moving forward and get rid of them.

"It's not me you should be apologising to, It's Zak," Bill retorted crossly.

"Sorry, Zak," I said, "do you mind if I examine you now?"

"Nah, nah Jimmy, that's not the way you talk to kids. You're in too much of a hurry. Kids need time. They don't like to be rushed, do they now my little Zakky Wakky?" he said as he tickled the child's toes. "You'd almost think you wanted rid of us the way you're talking.........." and he rambled on.

He was serious. He really did seem to think that he and Zak were the centre of my universe and I had all the time in the world for them. I realised the man had no insight into what a doctor could provide for him and his family, nor did he care. As far as he was concerned, I was there solely to cater for him and his son whenever it suited them. Anything outside that was of no interest to him. He was completely selfish and didn't play by the usual rules of society. I decided to dig my heels in. I'd had him and his son up to my back teeth.

"Look, Mr O'Keefe," raising my voice above his, "You've been in here already nearly half an hour. I have a lot of other patients to see. Now, I'm either going to examine Zak right this minute or I'm not going to examine him at all and you can take him to see another doctor." I could feel my face going bright red with the effort of keeping my temper. "I am not prepared to have a begging match with a two year old asking for his permission to examine him."

Bill looked shocked. I doubt if anyone had ever spoken to him like that before.

"Hey, who d'ya think you're talking to, Mr Wise Guy," he started.

"Mr O'Keefe," I shouted above him, "either I examine Zak right this minute or you can take him to another doctor. Now make up your mind."

Bill lumbered to his feet. He was a big man although he looked soft. I wondered what he was going to do. Was he going to get physical. He stood there clenching and unclenching his fat fists.

"Bill, Bill, please," a quiet, almost whimpering voice called out. It was Jane. "Please Bill. Just sit down and let's get Zak examined. It's him we're worried about isn't it? Please Bill for his sake, let's do it."

Bill sat down reluctantly and gave me a hostile stare. I doubted if he would ever call me Jimmy again. There was a frosty silence for a few seconds and then I said in my most business like tone, "Well then, let's get started. I'd like to look at Zak's chest if you don't mind pulling up his shirt."

Bill pulled up Zak's shirt without speaking revealing a fat little belly. Zak was caught off guard. He wasn't prepared for this speedy turn around of events. He looked in fury at me and then turned and looked at his father. Bill's face dropped with dismay. I thought he was going to lift Zak and run out of the room to save him the pain of being examined. Zak filled his lungs with air and started to scream. He screamed until he was purple in the face. "At least his lungs are one hundred per cent," I thought as I applied the stethoscope to his chest in a futile attempt to hear his heart.

I told Bill I had to examine Zak's abdomen and to do that, I needed him to lie down on the couch.

"There's no way this little guy's going to lie down on that cold couch," Bill said crossly.

It was on the tip of my tongue to ask him if he expected me to heat the couch up with a Bunsen burner but I didn't want any more arguments. I just wanted to get on and get finished with them.

"OK then. Can you lay him down across your knees please," I said.

It isn't a good way to examine a child but in the circumstances I would have examined him on top of a telegraph pole if it would have speeded things up. Reluctantly Bill laid his son across his knees. Zak twisted and squirmed and kicked out with both his feet. The good thing about it was Bill caught the full force of one of those kicks on the nose when he bent down to console his son with his coo-coo, I'm not going to let the bad doctor hurt you routine.

All I needed then was to look at his ears and throat. I always leave them to the last because it is the examination children like the least. I had sized up that Zak was in the front row when it came to protesting. I explained to Bill I needed to look at Zak's ear drums and he needed to hold him securely while I did so. I told him the auroscope would not hurt Zak unless he jerked his head about while I was examining him.

"Hold Zak firm and don't let him wriggle," I said as I instructed Bill how to hold his child correctly for an ear examination.

He stared at me with the same look of resentment on his face. "I hope you're not going to hurt him," he said and there was a threat in his voice.

"I've no intention of hurting Zak. Just hold him firmly the way I showed you and he won't be hurt in the slightest."

"The little guy doesn't like being held like that. I'll hold him this way," and he placed the boy over his shoulder and patted his back.

"I'm sorry, that's not a suitable way to hold a child for an ear examination. I could end up damaging his ear if I examined him in that position."

"No-one's going to damage my child," Bill said menacingly.

"I have no intention of damaging or hurting your child," I said shortly.

"I'm not holding him your way," Bill said.

"Well then, I won't be able to examine him. It's too risky."

Bill looked at me and I could see him thinking, "Zak's got to have his ears checked out but it's got to be done my way."

At that point, Jane chipped in.

"Oh, Bill," she said, "I do want Zak examined if only to put our minds at rest. Couldn't you maybe just think of holding Zak like the doctor says just for a wee minute? It's hard on the little thing with him being so unwell but it'll only be for a minute. It's better to be safe than sorry, isn't it darling?"

Eventually, after a howling match when Zak squirmed like a bag of worms, Bill agreed and I managed to get a look at both of his eardrums. They were normal.

"Now, can I just look at his throat?" and that was when the trouble started.

I knew it wasn't going to be a popular request. Zak was still crying from the indignity of having his ears looked at. His father looked at me angrily and Zak got the message. He let out a plaintive cry, a real put on job if ever I heard one. The noise was ear splitting but Zak still managed to keep that comforter firmly in his mouth the whole time.

"I thought the examination was over, Zak hates anybody touching his mouth," Bill shouted angrily.

"If he has a sore throat and I am to diagnose it, it's essential I look at his throat," I explained. It sounded logical to me so why was Bill looking so cross.

Maybe, Jane wasn't as timid as I thought. She drew Bill to one side and the two of them had a heated discussion. Zak had quietened down and was sitting there sizing up the situation. It was obvious from the way he was pursing his lips, he was ready to shriek. He knew something was up as he sucked harder on his soother to settle himself. He was sucking so hard, I was afraid he would swallow it

"Could you please take the soother out of his mouth please so I can look at his throat?" I asked when they came to an agreement that I was to be permitted to examine Zak's throat.

His mother looked at me in alarm. "We didn't think we would have to take his soother out. He gets very upset when we take it away from him. He even goes to sleep with it in."

"Couldn't you manage to examine him with it in?" Bill demanded.

"I'm afraid there's no way I could look down Zak's throat while he's sucking a big soother like that," I told them. Were these people for real I wondered.

They both stared at me with a look of complete consternation on their faces.

"You'd think I'd asked them to strangle their child," I muttered to myself.

I asked them if they weren't happy about my examining Zak's throat.

"We're not one bit happy about it," his mother snapped. She wasn't whispering now, in fact, she was coming close to shouting. I had the feeling she was close to tears as well. "Zak gets very, very upset when we take his soother away. He only has it out when he's eating."

"It will only be for a few seconds," I said patiently. "He can have it back straight away."

"But he'll scream. He always does when he gets upset."

"That's not a bad thing," I told her. "If he screams, he'll open his mouth and I'll be able to look down his throat at the same time."

The two of them didn't seem to think that was a good idea. They seemed oblivious of my presence as they discussed how they could deal with this new crisis.

"What'll we do, Bill?"

"I suppose we'll have to take the soother out, Jane. There doesn't seem to be any way round it. I don't like doing it though. Go on, you do it Jane."

"Oh no, Bill, I couldn't do that. You'll have to do it. You're the man in the family."

"Please, Jane. I don't want to hurt him. You know how upset he gets and he's been through a lot already. I don't want him blaming me for everything. You do it, please." All the fight seemed to have gone out of him. He sounded dejected.

I sat staring at them. I couldn't believe I was listening to such nonsense. It must have been the most ridiculous conversation I had ever heard in my life. An image of John Wayne dealing with the situation floated into my mind.

"O.K. Bill, you've got to do it. It's a dirty job but it's a man's job. You can't send a boy to do a man's job," and he swings his lassoo and catches hold of the comforter and pulls the thing out of Zak's clenched jaws, his horse whinnying and frothing at the effort of extracting the soother from Zak's clamped teeth.

The two of them were actually arguing about who was going to remove the soother. I felt like leaning over and yanking it out myself but thought I better not. Zak would scream and the parents would blame me. Eventually Jane agreed to take it our. She made soft little cooing noises as she approached Zak who was watching her suspiciously. She pulled gently at the soother.

Zak gritted his teeth like a hyena. She tugged. The child held on. It was obvious Jane was going to lose the battle even before she began.

"Please, Zak, be a good boy, just let your little soo-soo go. Please petsie, please."

Zak was having none of it. I almost began to admire him as he held onto the soother like grim death. At the same time, I was beginning to feel concerned he might bite through the soother and choke himself.

Bill was getting edgy. He was half out of his chair, his arms stretched out imploringly towards his wife. "That's enough, Jane. That's enough. Don't pull so hard. Take it easy. You'll hurt him. You're beginning to upset him. I think I know what to do. Leave it to me." Jane flopped back relieved, Bill was taking over.

He started to tickle Zak, trying to make him laugh so he would ease his grip on the comforter. He carried on for several minutes but it only made Zak more determined than ever to hang on. Bill tried pulling faces. That had no effect either. He offered him a biscuit but Zak wasn't interested.

"I don't know what to do. He won't let go," Bill sounded completely deflated. He was a beaten man.

I was fascinated by the behaviour of the two of them especially as I was sure there was nothing wrong with the child. I had forgotten my impatience and fatigue and the other long suffering patients in the waiting room. I was sitting back in my chair wondering how long this would go on and what would they try next. A small explosive device perhaps?

Finally Bill asked me what he should do.

"Carry on, Bill," I told him. "You're doing fine, just fine. Extra well in fact. It's only a matter of time. Just try and get that comforter out of his mouth. He's a determined little man isn't he? That can be a very healthy sign."

The two of them carried on for another ten minutes when Zak finally gave up. His jaw went into a kind of spasm and shortly after that, his mouth fell open. I took the opportunity to look down his throat. It was normal. His parents were leaning against the wall looking thoroughly exhausted as I reassured them. "Zak has a mild viral infection and he'll be quite alright in the morning."

They were too worn out to question my diagnosis. The three of them trooped out. Zak was the only one looking anyway normal with his teeth clamped firmly down on that soother again.

All the other patients had given up and gone home. The waiting room was empty. I sighed with relief. I was able to have my cup of tea and chocolate biscuit in peace and I needed it.

Clean Mad

Slievegart was a lively town. There was always something going on. There was a market once a week when farmers and fishermen poured in from miles around. Stalls were set up in the street and everything from boiled buttermint sweets to smoked salmon, ladies' flowery hats and second hand tractors were sold. Sometimes a mountain man would bring in a trailer load of sheep to be sold and there would be a lot of haggling before they all went to the pub to seal the deal. Bars put tables and chairs out on the pavements when the weather was fine.

I loved to drive slowly through Slievegart even when the market wasn't there to look at the old houses and the people. Quite a few locals recognised me after a couple of months particularly as I was driving Dr Roberts big red Landover. They would give me a cheery wave and shout something out like, "How's it going, Doc?" "Are you working hard or are you hardly working?" It gave me a feeling of belonging even though I'd only been there a short time and made me feel part of the community.

The town was built round a small bay. At either end of the town were terraced houses that had been built on the shore side of the road. The rest of the town had houses, shops, cafes and pubs on both sides of the main road, all painted in bright colours. Narrow lanes lead off the main street into a small maze of ancient houses.

I noticed all kinds of patterns of life evolving the longer I stayed. A group of old men would meet up in the town square and sit on a bench beside the fountain, chatting and smoking their pipes every morning. Yves, the French man would come out from his baker's shop at midday without fail and sweep the front door steps of the shop and the adjoining cafe and, often the pavement in front of them as well. Wearing a tall, white, chef's hat and a white apron, he would stand on the pavement, his arms akimbo and stare up and down the road as if he was trying to work out how many customers he might have for lunch that day. He would draw deeply on a Gauloise cigarette before returning to his shop.

The portly Parish Priest, Father Jeremiah O'Donovan who was renowned for his fondness of food, particularly cream buns, would be seen hurrying back to the parochial house as one o'clock approached, ready to discover what culinary delights his housekeeper had prepared for him. The postman ambled along the street, wheeling his bicycle more often than riding it, stopping to pass the time of day with everyone he met and the only policeman stationed in the town did his beat so regularly you could have set your watch by him.

I often saw a thin woman in her early thirties cleaning her door step in the middle of the day when I passed the terraced houses on the shore. She lived four or five houses down from Charlie O'Shea's. Twice a week, she would have a bucket and mop out and, with a lot of effort and enthusiasm, she would clean the pavement outside her house with a lather of suds.

I often thought, "Now that is one tidy woman if ever I saw one. If she keeps the inside of her house as clean as she keeps the pavement, I wonder what it looks like." When I saw the ferocity with which she tackled the stains on the pavement one day as I was passing, I began to think that maybe she was carrying things a bit too far. She almost seemed to be in a frenzy.

A couple of days after I had made those comments to myself, I was driving down the same road when I saw she had just started to mow the small patch of grass in front of her house or so I thought. She was bent over the machine and was working at a frenetic pace, I wondered what she was up to and slowed down a little to watch her.

Then I saw it wasn't a lawn mower she was using. It was her hoover. Was she really hoovering up the pieces of grass her mower had missed? That really was going too far. There's such a thing as being tidy but hoovering the lawn was over the top as far as I was concerned. I realized there must be something wrong with the woman.

I mentioned what I had seen to Hilda the next morning when we stopped for a tea break.

Hilda knew everything that was going on in Slievegart. She had been born and bred in the village. Apart from her nursing training at St Thomas's Hospital in London, she had lived all of her life in Slievegart – or all of it so far, as she liked to say.

She was a small plump woman with a jolly face and twinkling eyes. She always wore a dark blue nursing sisters uniform and a starched white nurses hat. Despite several offers of marriage, she had remained single. I think she felt she had a big enough family in the people of Slievegart. Hilda was one of the best nurses I ever met. She was kind, efficient, friendly, obliging, knowledgeable and humourous.

Her only real fault was the way she drove her green Morris Minor. She crawled like a snail with a limp around the country roads. I don't think she knew how to put the car into third gear. Fortunately there was hardly any traffic in Slievegart then or Hilda would have been the cause of many serious gridlocks.

"Oh, that woman. I know who you're talking about, Katie Delaney. She's been tidying like that for the last few years. She's the talk of the town with her tidying and she seems to have got a lot worse these last few months. I saw her, lifting the pebbles off her garden path and putting them into a bucket the other day. Apparently she washes them in hot water and soap once a month before putting them back on the path. She took to bringing a duster to Church with her and giving her pew a good cleaning before she sat on it. This cleaning business has gone too far and seems to have become some sort of a mania with her now."

"Has she any family?" I asked.

"She has indeed and the nicest, politest children you could ever wish to meet. She has four children. The oldest must be ten now and the youngest would be about two. The talk in the town is they're hardly allowed into the house in case they make it untidy. Apparently she makes them play outside in the back yard even when it's raining.

She doesn't like visitors in case they dirty the house. Everybody who visits has to take their shoes off, no matter who they are. If the Pope Himself called, she'd tell his Holiness to take off his white slippers and leave them outside. And when you do get inside, she follows you round with a mop in case you leave any marks on her polished floors."

"What does her husband think of it all?" I asked.

"Sure, he's never there. He's always away working. I think he worked hard when they were first married to earn enough money for them to have a decent standard of living. Now I think he works to keep away from Katie. Evidently, he can't even sit down in his own living room because he'll crinkle the cushions on the couch and that upsets Katie."

Two days later, Katie's husband, Joe Delaney phoned me soon after I'd finished morning surgery. He sounded tense.

"Look Doc," he said, "I've got to see you and it's about something very important. I don't like coming to the surgery because it's about my wife, I'm afraid someone would see me there and tell her. My life wouldn't be worth living if she found out I was talking about her. Is there any possibility you could see me when there are no other patients about? I'm at the end of my tether with this cleaning carry on of Katie's and so are the four youngsters."

Joe sounded desperate. I told him I would see him early the following afternoon. He was effusively grateful.

"If you can help me sort this out, Doc," he said, "I'll be grateful to you for the rest of my life."

Joe walked up to the surgery the following afternoon. He didn't come in his car in case anyone saw it parked outside. He was a neatly dressed, well built man in his early thirties. Beneath his tan, his face was drawn with anxiety.

He thanked me again for seeing him outside the usual surgery hours. Everything about him suggested a decent, hard working, reliable sort.

He sat staring in front of him and didn't seem too sure how to begin.

"You were saying you're having a bit of trouble with your wife and her cleaning," I prompted.

"Trouble, Doc, trouble's not the word, it's more than trouble. It's a living hell for me and the children living in that house with Katie and her cleaning. She's driving us mad. I'll tell you how bad it is for I'm so annoyed and depressed with her behaviour, I've had to stop myself driving my van over the cliffs into the sea to get away from it."

"Do you find her cleaning and tidying that bad, Joe?" I asked.

"Look Dr Griffin, I like a tidy house as much as the next man. I'm a tidy sort of person myself. I take my van in and wash it once or twice a week, keep it in proper order like. I know how to find any of my tools when I want them at a moment's notice and that's the way I like it but there's a limit to tidiness.

"The way it is now, I'd rather live in a pig sty with the children and have some peace of mind than live in that house of mine, the cleanest house in the whole of Ireland if not the entire world with all the tension that there is in it at the moment.

"I'll tell you how bad it is for the five of us though, to be honest, I haven't been fair on the poor children. I've started working longer and longer hours in the last couple of years to keep away from the house and my wife and her tidying so I can have some sort of peace. That leaves the little ones in the firing line instead of me and they get the brunt of her screaming and shouting about keeping the house tidy. I feel really bad about that.

"To tell you the truth, Doc, I can't take any more of her cleaning. I feel that if she tells me off one more time for leaving something untidy or making a mark on the floor, I'll get up and choke her and, God forbid, that's not me. I'm not a violent man but I just CAN'T STAND IT ANY MORE," and his voice rose to a roar. He buried his face in his hands and started to cry. He cried for a long time before he wiped his eyes with the sleeve of his coat.

"I'm sorry about that, shouting and then blubbing like a two year old," he said. "I can't remember when I last cried. It must have been thirty years ago but this has me completely beaten. Katie's turning me into a bad husband as well as a bad father. I don't stand up for the children any more. I don't think I can stand up for them in case I take a swipe at her in a fit of anger." and he burst into tears again and shook his head in despair.

"I don't know what to do. I just don't know what to do any more." He paused for a few minutes before continuing. "You don't know my wife and what's it like living with her with this cleaning mania she has but I'll try and explain. I'll run through the sort of things she gets up to. Then you can understand what sort of life myself and the children have.

"For a start, none of the children are allowed to have any of their friends over in case the friends dirty the house or make it untidy. As a result the kids are hardly ever asked anywhere because they never ask anyone back. That is the thing that gets me most of all, the fact the children and their development and their friendships are all being destroyed in the name of keeping a, rotten, horrible heap of stone and mortar tidy.

The children aren't allowed to lie or even sit down on their beds except at nights when they're going to bed in case they rumple the eiderdowns. Katie keeps them outside and makes them play in the back yard all day, no matter what the weather is like. Any time we sit down to eat, Katie is hovering over us waiting impatiently for us to finish so she can grab the dishes, wash them up and put them back in their place on the dresser. Then she will wash the table and dump the leftovers into the bin. No matter how tasty the food is or how much is left over, its straight into the bin. There's nothing in the fridge apart from a bottle of milk and a packet of butter and they're thrown out regularly too. It's not a home we live in, it's a shrine, a shrine to what?

She's been getting a lot worse over the last month or two. She used to get up at seven o'clock in the morning and that's early for these parts but she needed to get up then to get started because she has such a long list of thing to clean. This list has been getting longer and longer. She'd clean all day until she nearly fell down with exhaustion about ten or eleven o'clock at night. The weight has fallen off her over the years. She is that busy cleaning and scrubbing, she hardly finds time to cook for us or even eat herself.

"I'll often come home starving after a hard day's work to find there's no food ready and maybe the children gone to bed hungry. I can't go down to the chip shop every night. It's not good for myself and the children to be eating chips and burgers all the time and people notice those sort of things.

"It's hard enough earning a living without half the county talking about you, saying your wife is crazy. It affects my business too. Some people don't give me their business any more because they think there's something wrong with me too, not being able to control my wife and her cleaning."

Joe was getting everything off his chest. I couldn't have stopped him now even if I had wanted to. It was like a valve being released that lets off a huge amount of pressure.

"I was saying Katie used to get up at seven o'clock and start the tidying and cleaning then but I'll tell you what's happening now. She's getting herself up at five o'clock and is tidying until nearly midnight. You can't talk to her about it or try to reason with her. She listens to nothing and nobody. There's nobody can make her see sense.

"Her parents and brothers and sisters think she's crazy. When they tried to talk sense to her, she told them all to clear off and not come back. I put up with her, Doc, because I love her despite everything. I always have loved her ever since I was twelve years old and I love the children too even though I haven't been too supportive of them recently. I feel absolutely terrible about that which annoys me more than anything else. I know the Katie I'm living with now is not the Katie I married.

"There's something seriously wrong with her. She needs help. What's wrong with a woman who screams at you to take all the doors off the hinges once a month so that she can clean

92

them properly? I daren't refuse her or there'd be a dreadful scene. She uses a tooth-brush to clean the part of the door where the hinges are attached at least once a week.

"Another thing that really bugs me, I used to be a pigeon fancier. I kept pigeons from when I was no age. My father was the same. He loved racing pigeons with a passion. He was crazy about them and I took after him. The two of us got on great together but Katie made my life such a misery because of the pigeons that I had to give them up. She objected to their droppings and was prepared to do anything to stop them making a mess on the roof or anywhere near the house. She threatened to shoot or poison them so, in the end, it was easier to just get rid of them.

That affected the great relationship I had with my father. He thought I wasn't man enough to stand up to my own wife and that really annoyed me. And to think one of the things I liked about her when we were going out together was that she really liked pigeons nearly as much as I did until that cleaning craze got the hold of her."

"What was she like when you married her?" I asked. "Was she a bit over the top about keeping things clean then?"

"No, no, she wasn't, not at all. She was always a tidy sort of person from when I first knew her. She was tidy but not like she is now. If she had seen somebody doing what she does now when she was a young woman, she'd have laughed and thought they were mad. She even brings the pebbles in from the garden path so she can wash them once a month. Now, is that reasonable or am I the one going mad?"

"When did you notice things starting to change for the worse?" I asked.

"About five years ago, after Daniel was born. She started spending more and more time tidying up. Then, two years ago, when Elsie was born she got much worse but in these last two or three weeks she seems to have become like a maniac. If she goes on with this cleaning business much longer, she's going to collapse and die. She's only skin and bones as it is. Honestly,

Doc, I don't think any of us, including Katie, can take any more. When she's not tidying, she's planning her next day's tidying.

I'm sure you heard about her hoovering the lawn. It's the talk of the town and the children have to put up with all the teasing from the other children in the town about their mother being a crazy woman. Do you know something, she'd been at the hoovering business a lot longer than the last two or three weeks.

"She's been hoovering the side of the mattress where she sleeps for the last two years as soon as she gets up in the morning before she ever thinks of getting dressed. I lie in bed and try to sleep but she can't wait for me to get up so that she can hoover my side too. A couple of times when I've tried to have a bit of a lie in on a Saturday morning, she's turned the hoover on me and I've had to get up otherwise I think she would have hoovered my insides out."

Joe paused for breath, shaking his head despondently.

"Is there any mental illness in Jane's family?" I asked.

"Not a bit of it. They're all as sensible as the day is long except for her Dad. He's a bit demented."

"In what way?" I asked.

"He's a Liverpool supporter when everyone knows Newcastle United are the team of the future."

At least Joe hadn't lost his sense of humour.

"No, seriously Doctor, they're all fit and healthy, mentally anyway. They can't understand what's got into Katie any more than I can. Do you know something, Doc, and this would be funny if it was happening to anyone else but me. Katie has three hoovers, one for the clean work, one for the dirty work and one she keeps in reserve. What do you think of that - a three hoover family!" Joe laughed ruefully. "And do you know another thing? I don't think it will be long before she makes us all have a foot bath before we come into the house if things keep going on as they are. And I daren't even say it to her in a joke or she'd be straight down to the hardware store looking for one. After that, she'll want us to have a full body bath outside before we come into the house." Joe shook his head in despair. "What am I going to do at all Doctor? Is there anything you can do to help me?"

I was at a complete loss to suggest anything. With only one year's medical experience under my belt and two months working as a locum G.P. how could I help a woman who was seriously mentally ill and thinks there is nothing wrong with her and refuses to discuss her problems with anyone? Still, I had to come up with something. Joe was looking at me with imploring eyes, pleading with me to help him. It was no good telling him to come back another day or to wait until Dr Roberts came back. He needed help now.

"It's going to take a lot of time and work to get this put right," I said slowly. I was playing for time. My mind was a complete blank. I was waiting for some kind of inspiration to hit me. Then, slowly, it came to me. What was it Dr Roberts said as he drove off down the drive. "If you have any problems, give Dr O'Flahertie a call.

Dr O'Flahertie! That was the solution. I'd pass the buck to him, the whole hook, line and sinker and I'd get back to dealing with ordinary medical problems.

"Look Joe," I said unable to hide the relief from my voice although there was a nagging feeling in the back of my mind I couldn't put my finger on. "I think I know what I'll do to sort this matter out. I'll get Dr O'Flahertie to see Katie. He'll........"

Joe jumped as though I'd punched him in the teeth.

"Dr O'Flahertie," he roared, "are you serious, Doc? He's madder than my wife. I wouldn't let him near her with a barge pole never mind a medical opinion."

I knew what that little nagging doubt was now. It was Dr O'Flahertie.

"Why Joe, what's the matter with him? He's an excellent doctor and he's helped me with one or two clinical decisions in the last couple of months."

"What's wrong with Dr O'Flahertie, you ask me? What's right with him, is what I'd like to know? He knows as much about mental illness as Paddy Murphy's bullock. A neighbour of ours took a bad depression a few years back and wouldn't get out of bed....."

Why was all this starting to sound familiar to me.

"He was a lovely old man," Joe went on. "He'd been like an uncle to me but this depression he took was awful. He stopped talking or going out and wouldn't eat. The weight fell off him and he became as thin as a rake. He wouldn't let anyone send for the doctor. He hated troubling anyone.

In the end, O'Flathertie was sent for. Do you know what that lunatic did when he arrived at the house. He took one look at Johnny and said he had the cure for him. 'I've got the very cure for you, me boy,' were his words. Before we realised what was happening, he'd run out of the house and started lifting sods of turf off the stack in the back garden. He came back inside with them and started putting them under Johnny's bed.

"What are you doing, Doctor?" Johnny asked when he saw him taking out a box of matches and begin to strike them.

"I'd think that should be obvious to a man of your intelligence, Johnny," he said. "I'm lighting a fire under your bed."

"What?" was all the old man could say.

"Well, once it's lit, you can stay in your bed and burn or you can jump up and run for it."

"What did Johnny do?"

"Well Doc, Johnny was one of the most loveable, peaceful of men I ever met in my whole life. There was never a moment's trouble in him but something in the tone of O'Flathertie's voice fired him up, fired him up mightily altogether. He leapt out the bed like a goat with its tail on fire and ran over to his fireplace and grabbed his shot gun off the mantelpiece. He was looking for a cartridge to put in it when he heard the front door slam. He looked out of his window and there was O'Flathertie running like the hammers of hell for his car."

"Did Johnny get better after that?" I asked. I always liked to hear the ending to a story.

"Yes he did but not from O'Flathertie's line of treatment. He felt that seeing how he was out of bed he might as well go and see Dr Roberts. Dr Roberts gave him anti-depressants and he got better over time. But did you ever in all of your life hear of depression being treated like that, burning the patient out of his bed? It's like something from the Dark Ages and that's why I've no time for that man O'Flathertie."

I was in a real dilemma now. Who could I ask for advice? Maybe I should contact the local psychiatric unit but they were miles away and I didn't know anyone there.

"Look, Joe," I said. "I can't come up with a solution at this minute but I will try and find one by tomorrow. I'll make a few enquiries and sleep on it overnight if that's alright with you."

"I've had this problem with Katie for more than five years now. Another night won't make any difference."

I told him to phone me the next morning. He shook my hand and left.

As soon as he left I thought, "Well crazy or not, Dr O'Flathertie is the only other doctor I know so I'll have to go and see him and get his opinion. After all, Dr Roberts said he had a good clinical brain even if he is a bit eccentric."

I couldn't help wondering if there wasn't method in Dr O'Flathertie's madness. The same treatment he'd given Johnny might help Katie. A turf fire under her bed would probably burn her house down and then she wouldn't have a home to clean. Still, there had to be a better way than that.

I left to see Dr O'Flatherie straight away. It was a beautiful warm summer's day. As I drove past the row of terraced houses, I saw Katie out with her bucket and mop giving the pavement the third degree treatment. She really did look awfully ill. I drove up the rocky hill to Dr O'Flathertie's house and parked the Landover on the road. As I walked up the drive, I stopped and admired his luxuriant garden with its tropical plants and colourful blooms. An elegant lady in a blue cotton dress was tending one of the beds. She looked up and asked if she could help.

I told her I was Dr Robert's locum and was looking for Dr Flathertie.

"Ah yes, Dr Griffin," she said with a charming smile, "you're making quite an impression in Slievegart."

I wondered what sort of impression she meant.

"Sylvester's round the front of the house," she continued, "where the sun is. He's taking his R and R."

"R and R?" I queried.

"Rest and relaxation," she said with a tinkling laugh. "Sylvester's very fond of his R and R, very particular about it."

I went round to the front of the house and found the doctor lying on a reclining seat. He was wearing a pair of Bermuda shorts and a short-sleeved shirt of startling colours. A Panama hat shaded his face. There was a bottle of chilled white wine and a box of cigars close to his right hand. Dr O'Flathertie obviously took his R and R very seriously indeed.

I coughed and he screwed up his face so that his sunglasses lifted above his eyes.

"Well, well," he said, " if it isn't young Griffin on his rounds, Come on over here and sit yourself down and have a glass of this delicious little Chianti and tell me what all the folks in Slievegart are up to."

I pulled a wicker cane chair over beside him and sat down marvelling at the wonderful view he had of the coast and the sea from his patio.

"I won't have anything to drink thank you. I'm going back for the evening surgery."

"You will, you will, you will, you will," he insisted. "Of course you'll have a little drink. Take a drop of the Chianti. It will steady you up and put hairs on your chest and the evening surgery won't be a bother to you once you've had a couple of glasses."

I began to think my evening surgery would be completely pain free if Dr O'Flathertie had his way. I took a glass from him to save time and sipped it slowly.

"Get that drink down you, James," he said as he selected a cigar from the box and settled back in his chair. "There's plenty more where it came from. I don't suppose I could tempt you to a Monte Cristo cigar, could I James, a number four to be precise. It will last you nearly an hour while you're recounting your tale of woe."

"No thank you," I said, "smoking makes me nauseated."

"You're an awful man, James. Smoking makes you sick and drink makes you drunk. Maybe you should think about becoming a monk."

He clipped his cigar carefully with a gold clipper and rolled it between his middle finger and thumb and sniffed it like a bloodhound, before putting it into his mouth and lighting it. All conversation had ceased during this procedure. It was like a sacred ritual.

"Right, James," he said once he had the cigar lit, "I suppose you're here with one of life's great insolvable mysteries. Let's hear it from the master's mouth."

I told him the story from the beginning. He stared at me with his piercing brown eyes. Occasionally, a twinkle appeared in them. When I finished, he took an enormous puff from his cigar and blew the smoke out in a long leisurely stream.

"Do you know what's wrong with that lassie, James?" he asked.

"No," I said, "I don't"

"She's clean mad, clean crazy," and he laughed at his own humour.

I said nothing. I hoped he was going to come up with something better than that. I could hardly tell Joe what he had said particularly after the turf incident.

He put his fingers together and pursed his lips before continuing, "It's a tricky one alright, James. In a nutshell, this lady has developed a serious mental problem precipitated by the birth of her last two children. I think she needs to be admitted to a psychiatric hospital immediately.

"I remember her mother and one of her aunts both developed postnatal depression after the birth of their third child. Both went a bit odd but in a different way to Katie. They settled down on a course of anti depressants. Katie always was an anxious child from as far back as I remember her. I think the responsibility of keeping a house, a husband and three or four children was too much for her on top of having a propensity to post natal depression in the family history. That husband of hers a is a bit of an awkward boyo to live with too I'd imagine - a bit quick with the temper."

I raised my eyebrows. Was I going to get a different version of the turf story.

"He came after me with a shot gun one time quite a few years ago now when he was a young lad, after he disagreed with the treatment I'd given a neighbour of his, a man called Johnny who was suffering from a bad depression after drinking bucketfuls of bad poteen. That young thug. Delaney sent for me at four in the morning to sort out Johnny's problems. When I arrived he had a feed of drink in him and was cheeky with it. I can't imagine he'd be the easiest person in the world to live with. If you're going anywhere near his house, watch out for that gun of his." The incident with Johnny had obviously made an impression on Dr O'Flathertie too.

"I'll tell you what I think you need to do in this clinical situation, James." Dr O'Flathertie continued. "I think you need to go and see this young lady as soon as possible if she'll let you into the house and I don't think she will by the sound of her and explain to her and that lout of a husband of hers that she is seriously ill and needs to be admitted to a psychiatric hospital.

If she doesn't agree to go into hospital, you'll have to get a psychiatrist to come to her home and commit her. Let him do the dirty work like signing the committal forms for her compulsory admission. They get a big enough fee for doing it and the family can blame him if they don't like it. And mind and watch out for that man Delaney. If you see him reaching for his shooter, run for it."

Dr O'Flahertie advised me to get a psychiatrist called Dr Wright from the local psychiatric hospital to see Katie.

"He's the only one of them up there that's half sensible," he said. "As far as I can see, the rest of them are worse than the patients they look after."

Dr O'Flahertie held strong opinions.

As I left, he called out in a loud voice which must have echoed down to the town, "By the way, James, when that Delaney woman gets out of hospital, send her up here to do a bit of cleaning if she's any cleaning left in her. There's no cleaning in that wife of mine," and he pulled his panama back over his face and settled back in his lounger.

Mrs O'Flahertie looked up from her weeding as I went by, "I hope Sylvester made you a nice pot of tea, Dr Griffin," she said. "How's his R and R coming along? Is he at stage two, the bit where he pulls his hat over his head and says goodbye to the world for half an hour when interruption can only be made under pain of death?" And she laughed her merry laugh again.

"Everything seems to be going to plan on the R and R front," I said with a smile, wondering as I walked on how such an oddball as Dr O'Flahertie managed to get himself such a pleasant, charming wife.

Joe Delaney called the following morning.

"You know Joe," I said, "I've been thinking a lot about Katie and talking to one or two medical people and, from a medical point of view, we think her case is serious. You were telling me yesterday she's hardly eaten or taken anything to drink over the last three or four days. I happened to be going past your house yesterday and I noticed her outside. She has lost an awful lot of weight since I last saw her and she looked dreadful."

"What are you saying, doctor?" Despite his politeness, there was an air of impatience about Joe. Thoughts of the scene with the shot gun danced before my eyes.

"I'm saying if she goes on the way she's going, not eating or drinking, she'll end up collapsing. I think she has to go into hospital as soon as possible for her own welfare."

"There's no way she'll agree to go into hospital and leave that house of hers."

"If a consultant advises her to go, she'd have to consider it."

"If God Himself told her to go to hospital to save her life, she'd still say no and tell Him not to come back unless He took His shoes off first and brought a mop with Him."

I didn't want to rush it and tell Joe we might have to get his wife committed to hospital, sectioned was the old word, as an involuntary patient. When you get to that stage, it always comes as a shock to both the patient and the relatives, no matter how ill the patient is, that the patient is going to be forcibly removed from their home and detained in a hospital for an indefinite period whether they like it or not.

"Still Joe, if a consultant was of the opinion Katie needed to go to hospital for her own safety, do you not think she would be better going?" I said as gently as I could.

"What do you mean exactly, Doc?" Joe asked abruptly.

"I mean, Joe, your wife is very, very ill. She is on the verge of collapsing and maybe making herself permanently ill. We've got to think of that, the risk she's putting herself to and the fact she seems to have no insight in to what she's doing. Katie may have to go into hospital whether she likes it or not."

"Are you telling me you're going to put my wife in a mental hospital against her will?" Joe was cross now.

"No, not exactly........"

"Well then, what are you telling me?"

This was harder than I expected.

"I'm saying your wife needs to be seen and assessed by a consultant psychiatrist today or tomorrow at the latest. He is an expert in these matters. He will form his own opinion about whether she has to go into hospital or not, whether she needs to be rehydrated because she hasn't been drinking for several days in this heat and whether she needs to go to a general hospital or a psychiatric unit for her rehydration."

"There's no way she'll agree to an assessment by anybody," Joe stated.

"We need to think of your wife's long term welfare at this stage, Joe. If she collapses from dehydration or fatigue she would have to go to hospital anyway and we might have left it too late. She might have damaged her kidneys by then for example."

"How will you get a psychiatrist to assess her?" Joe interrupted.

"I'll phone him this afternoon and arrange for him to call at your house tomorrow afternoon. I'll call to see your wife myself in the meantime, tomorrow morning, to see if there's any possibility she'll agree to go to hospital herself without getting a psychiatrist involved.."

"She'll never agree to that and anyway, that's no good to me," Joe interrupted again. "She'll blame me for sending for you and I'll get it in the neck for the next ten years."

"She won't blame you because I'll tell her I saw her myself in the garden with the hoover and thought she was overdoing it and I was very worried about her and that Hilda, the district nurse, had expressed concern to me about her as well."

"She won't let you in."

"Whether she lets me in or not doesn't matter. I'll be back with the psychiatrist in the afternoon if she doesn't. It's him, in the end, who will decide what is to be done. It is not a decision he'll make lightly. There's a lot of legal implications involved in taking this sort of decision and it is always made with the patient's best interests in mind. For Katie's sake and the children's, we have to act on it.

Reluctantly, Joe agreed. He said he'd phone me at the surgery the following lunch time to see what was happening.

I phoned Dr Wright that afternoon. He was the most abrupt man I ever spoke to in my life.

"Hello," I said and introduced myself.

"Yes?" he replied.

"Yes what?" I wondered.

The phone remained silent for several seconds. I thought the line had gone dead.

"Hello, hello, are you still there?" I asked

"Yes, What do you want?"

"I'd like you to visit a patient of mine."

"What's the name?"

"Dr Griffin."

"No, no, the patient's name?"

"Oh, ah, Katie Delaney, her...."

"Address?"

"Patient's address?"

"Who else?"

I gave him her address.

"Married?"

"Yes"

"Husband's name?"

"Joe."

"Children?"

"Yes."

"How many?"

"Four. She got ill after the birth of her last two children," I managed to say before he pounced again.

"Date of birth?"

I scrambled to look for it amongst the notes and read it out.

"What's wrong with her?"

"Well over the last five years she has been cleaning to an obsessional degree and.........."

"T.M, I."

"T.M.I." I repeated.

"Yes, T.M.I., too much information. Obsessional cleaning you say. Is she on any treatment?"

"No, she won't see a doctor."

"Past history or family history of mental illness?"

"Her mother and an aunt had some form of post natal depression but not as serious as Katie's. Katie had been completely normal up to the birth of her last two children."

"What is Dr O'Flathertie's opinion?"

I was impressed. Apart from not wasting any time, this man Wright understood the value of Dr O'Flatherties local medical expertise, despite his eccentricities.

"He thought she needed hospital admission.

"Involuntary committal, I presume he felt?"

"Yes."

"Good. I'll be at your practice tomorrow afternoon at half past two sharp. Thank you for the referral. Goodbye," and the phone went dead.

I took a deep breath. I thought psychiatrists were supposed to take things nice and easy, slow and slower were meant to be their two speeds. That man Wright was like a whirlwind. He left me feeling drained the way he extracted information. He should have been a surgeon cutting bits out of people if he possessed that sort of incisiveness.

The following day I went down at midday and tried to talk to Katie. She was outside mopping her front door step. As soon as I put my foot on the path, her face clouded over with irritation. "More work for me," I could see her thinking.

"What do you want?" she asked sharply.

"Maybe she and Dr Wright will get on well together after all," I thought to myself. "They both have the same abrupt way with them."

"I'm Dr Griffin, I've dropped in to see you. I saw you in the garden yesterday and thought you didn't look well"

"You'll not be seeing me. I don't need no doctor," she replied crossly before going into the house and slamming the door behind her. It was the quickest home visit I ever did.

A highly polished black Jaguar drove up Dr Roberts drive at half past two exactly that afternoon and came to an abrupt halt outside the front door The car had hardly stopped before a nimble man of forty, with short black hair and dressed in a dark suit leapt out of it and half ran and half walked over to me.

"Dr Griffin?" he asked. "I'm Dr Wright."

After a perfunctory hand shake, he fixed his eyes on me and gave me his total attention. Somehow it made me like the man immediately. He looked professional in his dark suit, white shirt and college tie. I felt a bit under dressed in my short sleeved shirt and khaki trousers. Dr Wright was one of those rare people you sometimes meet who inspire you with confidence. I knew instinctively he would do his best for Katie, even if his manner of doing it might be a bit unusual.

"My car," he said, marching over to the Jaguar.

I got into a spotless car that smelt of walnut and leather and sank into the softest seat imaginable. With one swift movement that took me by surprise, he had the car turned round and we were heading down the avenue to the town as if preparing for take off.

"The town I presume," he said.

I nodded my head. Dr Wright raced down the road until he had to slow down for a tractor and trailer that was plodding along at fifteen miles an hour. Even Dr Wright had to see it was too dangerous to try and pass on those bends. For a man of few words, he said a lot then.

"Get out of my road you complete moron," he screamed at the farmer who didn't even know we were behind him and couldn't hear him anyway. "Why don't you pull that heap of scrap into the side of the road and let me past, you stupid excuse for a donkey brain. If brains were dynamite, you wouldn't be able to blow your nose. You total imbecile!" I was completely taken aback. Dr Wright was ahead of his time with his display of road rage

He blasted his horn as we eventually did pass and sped on screeching to a halt outside the Delaney house. He ran up the path and started banging the heavy door knocker repeatedly. I'd told him on the way down Katie had refused to see me that morning.

"We'll see about that," was all he said.

Nobody answered the door and he kept banging it, louder and louder until people came out from the neighbouring houses to see what the commotion was. Then Katie suddenly swung the door open.

"What is your problem, you crazy lunatic," she screeched at him, her eyes seeming to bulge almost out of her head. She was very, very angry and looked very disturbed.

"I'm Dr Wright. I'm a psychiatrist and I've come to see you. I haven't much time and I'm coming in," and he pushed his way into the hall.

"You're not coming into my house, no matter who you think you are. Take your shoes off when you stand in my hall way."

She was livid. She bent down and tried to pull Dr Wright's shoes off. The fact he wore shoes in her hall way seemed to annoy her more than the fact he had pushed his way in.

"Where is your husband, Mrs Delaney?"

"Get out of my house and get your shoes off in my hall way," she shouted as she struggled to get at Dr Wright's feet. I was impressed by the way he managed to fend her off. Maybe he was used to patients attacking his feet.

"You need to go to hospital today, Mrs Delaney," he said firmly.

That stopped her for a second or two, then she became angrier than ever.

"Who do you think you are, telling me I need to go to hospital? Get out of my hallway you stupid little squirt. You're dirtying my house."

"You're going to hospital today, Mrs Delaney and that's final either as a voluntary patient or as a non voluntary patient so you'll have to make up your mind which it is to be and make it up quickly.

I had reckoned with his abruptness it would take Dr Wright five minutes to interview Mrs Delaney and make up his mind about her. I hadn't reckoned on him taking thirty seconds, I had told Joe to call home around about three o'clock. Fortunately Joe turned up early.

"Mr Delaney" Dr Wright said. "I'm a psychiatrist. I have just examined your wife. She is very ill and needs to be admitted to a psychiatric hospital at once for several weeks, maybe longer."

Joe was shocked by the rapid turn of events but Dr Wright spoke with such confidence and conviction. I could see Joe was impressed.

"Your wife can decide to come in as a voluntary patient and if she refuses, we will have to section her and take her to hospital forcibly for her own health and safety. I'll give you a minute to talk to her." He looked at his watch and walked out.

"I have found," he said turning to me, "that if the patient or their relatives can't make up their minds about admission in one minute, they never can."

One minute later he marched back up the path.

"What is it to be?"

"I'm not going to no hospital and that's final." Katie screamed. Joe opened his hands wide to show he was helpless in making her change her mind.

"That's unfortunate" was all Dr Wright said. Turning to Joe he said "I'll be back in half an hour with an ambulance and three Gardai. Have some clothes packed for you wife.

He turned and indicated to me to follow him as we went to his car and drove back to Dr Roberts house.

He phoned for an ambulance and then contacted the Garda station in a nearby town.

I need two strong men down here immediately Sgt Brannigan," he said, "to help Garda Molloy of Slievegart remove an ill woman from her house and escort her to the Psychiatric Unit." There was a lot of mumbles and explanation from the other end of the line.

"An hour and a half is no good to me Sergeant. The ambulance is already on its way."

Sgt Brannigan was obviously not pleased with Dr Wright. I heard what sounded like a very cross mumble.

"That is unfortunate, Sgt Brannigan," Dr Wright replied. "I will hold you personally responsible if anything happens to this lady in the interim and will inform your superiors of my dissatisfaction with the service you provide for the mentally ill." He put the phone down and turned to me and smiled.

"That should ensure the reinforcements I require," he said.

We went back to the Delaney house. The ambulance was just drawing up. Fifteen minutes later, two cross looking gardai drove up. By then the garda Molloy had arrived as well. We all marched up the path.

Katie appeared at the door looking distraught. When she saw how many people were on her path, she came running at us screaming at the top of her voice. "Get your big clumsy boots off my path, you horrible men. Get off my path right now. Look at the marks you've made."

Dr Wright walked straight up to her.

"Mrs Delaney. I have five big, strong men here" and he nodded to the three Gardai and the two ambulance men. "They are going to bring you to hospital one way or another. There is an easy way of doing this which means you just walk down the path with us and there is a hard way where we carry you down the path. Believe me, for your own sake and for our sake, please walk down the path."

"I'm walking down no path. I'm not leaving my house for the likes of you to walk all over it in your filthy hob nailed boots." She turned to go up the path again. Her husband and children were at the door looking distressed as they watched the poor, agitated woman make a last pathetic stand.

Dr Wright nodded and the five men sprang into action. They surrounded her and she immediately started hitting the nearest one on his chest with her fist in a futile attempt to delay them taking her away.

The men gently took a grip on her arms and marched her down the path as she screamed and screamed. More of her neighbours and passers by had come to see what the fuss was about with the ambulance and the gardai arriving and all the noise. There was quite a crowd looking on. It was an extremely distressing and humiliating moment for the family but there was no other way of dealing with someone in such a bad mental state who needed help and wouldn't accept it.

The doors of the ambulance were closed and it sped off.

Dr Wright turned to me.

"Very unpleasant affair for all concerned Dr Griffin. No other way though. She has puerperal psychosis and severe obsessive compulsive illness. In patient treatment for six to twelve weeks. Outlook with a supportive husband like Joe is reasonably good though it will take time. Tell Dr O'Flathertie, well done."

He shook my hand, got into his car and drove off at great speed.

The Gate and the Bucket

"Hello, is that the doctor?"

"Yes it is," I replied.

"Well this is Mrs Scullion of Cloonmeenan speaking. You've got to come up to my house as soon as you can and speak to my wee Jimmy and stop him jumping off the high gates." It was a pleasant old woman's voice on the phone. She sounded anxious. I presumed she was worried about her grandson's behaviour.

"Can you not get wee Jimmy to stop jumping off the gates yourself, Mrs Scullion?" I asked.

It was hardly a medical problem, more one of discipline.

"Ah, there's no talking to my wee Jimmy. He's very headstrong and nobody can stop him from doing anything when he puts his mind to it."

I was a bit surprised at her comment. Children were usually obedient to their parents and even more so to their grandparents in the 1970s. They weren't all angels by any means but they had been brought up to respect authority. Wee Jimmy seemed ahead of his time with that rebellious streak of his.

"Could you not get his father to have a word with him and maybe discipline him.

"His father's been dead this long time and besides, wee Jimmy's too old to heed anybody."

"Too old! Why, how old is he?"

"He's 76 on his next birthday."

"76," I repeated in astonishment. I thought you were talking about a child."

"No doctor, I'm talking about my husband although sometimes I wonder if he isn't still a child the way he carries on. Jimmy will be 76 on his next birthday in two weeks time if he doesn't kill himself before it with all this gate jumping business of his."

"And when did he start jumping off gates, Mrs Scullion?"

"About sixty years ago."

"Sixty years ago!" This conversation was beginning to sound bizarre.

"Why didn't you call the doctor before now?"

"Because I never had to. He didn't do the jumping that often before, maybe three or four times a week then but over the last two or three weeks, he's at it day and night. I'm afraid he's going to hurt himself especially when he jumps in the dark."

"Why does he jump off gates in the first place?" I asked.

I could understand young lads jumping off gates for fun or for dares but most boys had given up that sort of activity by the time they had reached their teens and certainly by their mid seventies.

"He says it makes him feel better."

"What way does it make him feel better?"

"He doesn't say. Jimmy's not a great one for the talking. He just tells me he has to do it and some days he says he has to do it more than others. He says it makes him feel right."

"Right?"

"Aye right is what he says. Lately he's taken to jumping off higher and higher gates and he's even jumping off the pillars now. I'm scared he'll hurt himself when he lands and fracture his hips or something."

I was at a loss to explain this extraordinary behaviour. Had Jimmy gone completely mad or had he developed some sort of dementia. Maybe he had taken a small stroke that had knocked off part of his brain – the part that stops you jumping off gates.

"O.K, Mrs Scullion. I'll see what I can do. Can you get Jimmy to come into the surgery this evening and I'll try to get to the bottom of this."

"Jimmy won't come to the surgery, doctor. Wild horses couldn't drag him there. He'd rather die first."

"Has he a problem about coming to the surgery?"

"He says he's never put a foot inside a doctor's surgery in his entire life and he's not going to start now. He said his Uncle Jack went down to the dispensary sixty years ago as fit a young man as ever walked through the town of Slievegart and feeling as

112

right as rain. The Dispensary doctor took one look at him and sent him straight to a T.B. ward in Tralee Hospital. Jimmy's Uncle Jack was dead within the month."

I'd heard stories like that before and they were pure nonsense. If Uncle Jack's medical records could have been unearthed, they would almost certainly have shown that he had some advanced form of tuberculosis – probably riddled with the disease and with no treatment available in those days his outlook was hopeless – hospital or no hospital.

"There's another one or two things I think I should maybe mention about Jimmy." Mrs Scullion continued. "I know some of the neighbours think what he does is odd, though I don't see it that way myself what with my living with him for near on sixty years."

"What are the other things he does, Mrs Scullion?"

"Well, Jimmy likes to stick his head in a bucket of water from time to time," Mrs Scullion went on.

"Stick his head in a bucket of water!"

Jimmy must be roaring mad. I'd have to get Dr Wright to sort him out straight away.

"Yes doctor, and the bucket is full of cold water. He has buckets of cold water left all around the farm and out in the fields and when he feels the notion on him, he puts his head into the nearest bucket.

"And how long does he keep his head in the bucket when he does that?" I asked.

"About half a minute and, if when he's in the notion, sometimes for a full minute. There's another thing he does as well that people think is strange."

What other strange thing does he do, Mrs Scullion?"

I dreaded to think what else he would be doing, a seventy six year old jumping off gates and pillars that must be six or eight feet high and putting his head in a bucket of cold water was hard enough for me to contend with.

"Well, we got an electric fence about five or six years ago to keep some heifers from breaking out. Jimmy says if he grips the fence until he nearly passes out, it makes him feel better."

"And would he do that often, Mrs Scullion?"

"He electrocutes himself about once or twice a month. Jimmy says he's not too fond of the electrocution end of things, too painful by half is what he says. Now doctor do you think you'll be able to come up and stop him jumping off the gates and pillars. It's that what's worries me the most."

Going from her description of Jimmy I didn't think I'd be capable of making him do anything he didn't want to do.

"Have you any family, Mrs Scullion?" I asked.

"Aye, six boys and two girls."

"And what do they think of Jimmy's behaviour."

"Nothing."

"Nothing!" I said. "Don't they find it a bit odd?"

"No, not at all. Didn't they grow up with it since they were young. One of them does the same thing himself."

"They must be a bunch of maniacs trying to break their legs or electrocute themselves," I thought.

"And why does your son do these things? Did he ever explain that to you??"

"He says it makes him feel right."

"I don't suppose he told you what way it makes him feel right."

"He hasn't told me so far. He's like his father, not a great one for the talk"

"I saw him and Jimmy having a long chat out in the fields one day a lot of years back and after that, this son of mine, Joseph, started doing the same antics – jumping off gates and putting his head in buckets."

I had never come up against anything like this before in my life or even heard of anything that remotely resembled it. I was totally perplexed. Not for the first time I wondered if doing Dr Roberts locum had been such a good idea.

"OK Mrs Scullion, I'll come up this afternoon and see if I can sort something out, though I can't promise anything."

"That'll do very nicely Dr Griffin and thank you kindly," Mrs Scullion said as she put the phone down.

At tea break that morning, Hilda was giving out about what she called a BTA who had come to the village for a two week holiday and was causing her no end of trouble. The BTA had sent for her twice already, to check his child's temperature.

"What's a BTA, Hilda?" I asked.

"A BTA, James, is a class of being you find in Ireland from time to time. Most of them are far too big for their boots and think they're a cut above the rest of us."

"But what does BTA stand for, Hilda?"

"It stands for 'Been To America', James, 'Been To America'. There's a bad case in town at the moment who thinks the rest of us are a bunch of repressed stay at home dinosaurs."

I thought I had an inkling who Hilda might be talking about and decided to change the subject as quickly as possible before she tried to involve me. I mentioned Jimmy to her and his gate jumping antics.

She laughed and laughed until I had to slap her on the back.

"Well, that's a good one," she said, "Jimmy's as odd as two left feet but one of the nicest men you could ever meet. His wife Sara's a lovely woman too but as peculiar as they come. She goes to bed with her boots on in the winter. They live up in the hills in a remote wee cottage. I don't know how they managed to rear their family on their small plot of land but they did and they're as nice a family as you could ever hope to meet.

"They got electricity five or six years ago but they still light the Tilley lamp at night. One of their neighbours who drops in on them, told me they sit by the turf fire all evening and sometimes most of the day, just looking into the embers and saying nothing. The neighbour said that every so often Jimmy gets up and without speaking, goes into a corner of the room, kneels down and puts his head into a bucket of water and holds it there for about a minute. Then he gets up again, without drying his head or saying a word and goes back to his seat. The wife doesn't even look up. Still they seem as happy as can be together. Maybe not talking is the key to their successful marriage."

"And does anybody know why Jimmy puts his head in a bucket of water?" I asked.

"Nobody has a notion. If anyone asks him he just politely tells them it makes him feel right. If you can solve that mystery, James, you'll be a good 'un," and Hilda started laughing again. At least my problem had made somebody happy.

That afternoon, I set off in the Landrover up into the Kerry hills. It was a beautiful cloudless day with a soft breeze blowing in from the Atlantic. I put Bonnie in the front passenger seat and she barked with excitement at the prospect of a trip out. She loved a run in the Landrover, her head out of the window and the wind ruffling her face.

Hilda had given me directions to the Scullion's cottage. Hilda was a great nurse, one of the best I ever met but she hadn't a clue about directions.

"You'll come to a little trickle of a stream running across the road," she said "and about fifty yards past that, you'll see a fork in the road. Take the right fork and go up there two hundred yards and the house is straight in front of you on the right."

Straight in front of you on the right? What did that mean exactly? I wondered but I didn't like to question her too closely.

After twenty minutes of driving along narrow, twisted roads and old stone bridges and through several flocks of sheep lying on the road, I came to a large stream that was tumbling down from a small waterfall and gushing across the road. Was that the little trickle of a stream Hilda had been referring to or was the little trickle further on up the road?

I drove on slowly looking for a stream or a house. After nearly half a mile, I came to a fork in the road – a triple fork. Which fork was I to take? I tried the one on the right. It got narrower and narrower and after a mile, petered out into a bog track and then into the bog itself. There was nowhere to turn the Landrover.

I had an awful job reversing a mile backwards and nearly toppled into the bog several times. The sun was blazing down and the sweat was lashing off me. I had a dreadful pain in my neck from constantly looking backwards. Bonnie had spotted some rabbits running over the bog and had gone crazy with excitement. I had to let her out before she drove me round the bend with all her noise.

By the time I got back to the triple fork, I had been on the road nearly an hour. I hadn't even found the patient's house nor had I a clue how I was going to deal with his bizarre symptoms when I did. I was beginning to worry about being back in time for the evening surgery.

I took the middle fork and after a mile, came upon a neat whitewashed cottage with a thatched roof and red painted doors and window frames.

Bonnie was covered in mud after chasing across the bog and I hadn't let her back into the Landrover. She ran behind barking excitedly. When we approached the cottage, three black and white collies raced out to meet us. They crowded around Bonnie yelping with delight at meeting a new friend. Their noise brought a small, wiry, old man to the door of the cottage.

"Shut up and come over here, you stupid dogs," he shouted good naturedly at them and gave a sharp whistle. The collies immediately turned and ran back to him, their tails wagging furiously.

"Well" I thought, "there can't be too much badness or madness in a man that can command that sort of obedience and love from his dogs."

"What can I do for you young man?" he asked in a soft brogue as he came over to me. "Are you lost? There's not many makes their way up here unless they've taken the wrong road."

I thought for someone who wasn't meant to be chatty, Jimmy was doing very well for himself.

"No actually, I'm not lost Mr Scullion. My name is Dr Griffin. Your wife asked me to call."

"Did she now," he said with a twinkle in his eye. "She never said there was anything wrong with herself. Breakdown in communication I think is the term they use nowadays, Doc," and he laughed.

There was something very nice about this old man with his kind face and twinkling blue eyes that looked as if they were always about to laugh.

"Is that your dog?" he asked as Bonnie crept up the yard to try and rejoin the Collies.

"It's Dr Roberts' dog actually but I like to take her around with me."

"She's a lovely looking retriever," he said looking at her "but a bit on the dirty side. Come on over girl," he called and to my surprise, Bonnie sprang towards him.

"You're looking very dirty, my girl, aren't you after all that rolling around in the bog enjoying yourself? You can't go home in the doctors motor looking as dirty as that. Can you?" He had a way of speaking to Bonnie that seemed to delight her. She wagged her tail furiously and gave short excited barks as she stared at him almost in adoration. "I've the very thing for you as it happens," and he reached over and lifted a bucket of water from behind a low stone wall. I thought for a moment he was going to dunk his head into it.

"Sit down there now quietly girl and don't move," he commanded.

Bonnie sat down beside him and he poured the bucket of water slowly over her head and down her body. To my amazement, Bonnie didn't move. When he finished he said "Off you go now girl and dry yourself." Bonnie ran off into the middle of the yard and shook herself dry.

"While I'm at it, are you alright for a bath yourself doctor?" Jimmy said with a chuckle.

"Oh I'm fine thank you Mr Scullion, all the same" I replied.

As I spoke, his wife came to the door. She was a plump old woman with a motherly face and kindly eyes.

"I've got the doctor up to see you, you old mutt," she called out in a good natured hectoring tone to her husband. "He's going to check you out for brains to see if he can find any and after that, he's going to try and stop you jumping off gates and pillars."

Jimmy looked at me with a smile. "Never marry an interfering woman, doctor. They'll be the bane of your life."

"Never mind him, doctor," Sara replied "he's never spoken a word of sense since the day and hour I met him. You can't cure that but come on inside and see if you can cure that gate jumping craze of his."

Jimmy laughed at her feigned crossness. They had a bantering teasing relationship which was lovely to watch. Each one was delighted when they got one over on the other but equally happy when the other came back with a better answer.

Jimmy showed me into the cottage. It was like walking into the past. The floor was made of large slabs of granite that had been worn smooth by centuries of being trodden upon. A turf fire with orange embers glowed in the middle of a large stone hearth on one wall. It gave the welcoming smell of turf to the room. There was a comfortable armchair on either side of the fire and a large wooden bench along one wall where the children must have sat. A blue painted dresser leant against another wall. It was full of shining delph, speckled and white and blue and brown. Colouful patterned cups were suspended from small hooks on the dresser shelves. There were religious pictures hanging on every wall and a large St Brigid's cross made of reeds on the mantel piece.

As I surveyed the room I spotted a white enamel bucket full of water tucked into one corner of the room beside the dresser. Was it one of his dunking buckets, I wondered?

"Have a seat and take the weight off your feet," Jimmy said as he pulled a wooden chair out from under a table.

I sat down as Sara and Jimmy settled into their armchairs.

"Now, what can I do you for, doctor?" Jimmy asked.

"Well Mr Scullion. It's like this. Your wife phoned me to say she was very concerned about how often you have taken to jumping off gates and pillars lately."

"Very concerned did you say doctor?" Jimmy repeated.

"I said a bit concerned Jimmy, for your information, not very concerned, a very, very small bit concerned," Sara retorted.

We all laughed.

"Now, Mr Scullion," I continued, "as you know, jumping off heights at your age is not without its risks. That's probably why most men, as they get on, stop doing it."

"Is that a fact, doctor?" Jimmy said laughing.

"It is indeed, Mr Scullion and your wife wants me to get you to stop jumping off gates and pillars. Now my problem is, and I need your help here – is there anything you can think of that I can say or do to you to stop you jumping off pillars and gates, apart from tying you up?"

Jimmy chortled. "Maybe tie the Missus up or gag her to stop her interfering doctor, is my best suggestion."

Jimmy looked and sounded a lot more humorous and sensible than most men I had ever met. My theory of him having a serious mental problem had long gone out of the window. Dr Wright wouldn't be able to bail me out of this one. Still, I wondered what on earth made such a normal looking man like Jimmy do such peculiar things.

"Could you at least try and explain to me, Mr Scullion, what jumping off gates and ducking your head in buckets of water does for you?"

Jimmy hesitated for a moment before shrugging his shoulders as if to say, 'what have I got to lose.'

"I'm not a man who likes talking too much or complaining," he began, "or listening to too many complaints either, for that matter doctor…"

"If you don't mind me interrupting Mr Scullion, it's a good job everybody isn't like you or myself and a whole lot of other doctors would be out of a job."

"There's no fear of that happening, Doctor," Jimmy said with a laugh. "When I go down to Slievegart to the Friday market, I hear so many of the old timers going on about their bad health and their complaints that it's a treat to get back to the quiet of my wife and the peace of the hills where the only sound is the cry of the curlew and the wind rustling through the reeds."

"Get on with you Jimmy and all your fancy poetry talk," Sara said sharply, "and tell the doctor what you've been up to over the years with all those silly antics of yours, jumping off gates and the likes of it. I've waited nearly sixty years to hear why you do them and my curiosity is nearly getting the better of me now."

Jimmy laughed again. "You always were a nosy one, Sara, pestering me with all your questions about the gate jumping. That's the second time now you've asked me on fifty eight years of marriage."

"Aye well, I hope your answer this time is a bit more sensible than it was last time I asked you."

"Why? What did he answer then?" I asked.

"He said he did it because he felt like it and if I felt like it, I should do it as well."

"I was witty then," Jimmy said with a broad grin.

"Well go on and tell us then Jimmy. I've waited long enough. Don't keep me waiting until I'm turned eighty or I'll maybe be dead and never hear the answer."

"Alright, alright, I'll tell you then, you nagging old woman if I'm going to get any peace in my own home" he said. He paused and took a long breath. "All my life, as far back as my teenage years, I have had what I can only call a fuzziness in my chest as if there were butterflies in there that have been let loose. Sometimes the butterflies lasted for a few minutes, sometimes they went on for an hour or more and sometimes the fuzzy feeling went on for days. If I walk a lot or drink strong tea or take a couple of pints on market day, it makes the butterflies worse. I had to give up smoking years ago because it brought on those butterflies something shocking.

121

"It all started one fine day when I was a young lad of about fourteen or fifteen. It came and went a few times that week and I got very vexed with it. I remember I was going home through a field one evening and had to climb over a high gate. I jumped off the top of it and, to my surprise, the butterflies that had started an hour earlier stopped. I experimented after that. Every time I got the butterflies I found jumping from a high gate put them away.

Another time, me and some other young lads were mucking about in the river. We had a competition to see who could hold their breath the longest under water. I had a dose of butterflies that day that had been going on for a long time and I found holding my breath like that under water put them away, It was a great relief."

"And is that why you hold on to the electric fence?" I asked "because it puts the butterflies away?"

"Aye, that's right although I'm not too fond of that end of things. I only do that as a last resort if nothing else will stop the butterflies."

"And how did you find out that an electric shock helped?" I asked.

"That's a long story if you've got the time to listen, doctor," Jimmy said.

I nodded. I was late for the surgery already, a few more minutes wouldn't matter.

"There's a man who lives in a big house down in Slievegart called Swinson," Jimmy began. "He owns a stud farm. Swinson is a bit of joker and a smart Alec although he runs his farm efficiently enough. He was the first farmer in these parts to get an electric fence long before anyone hereabouts had even heard of them. Swinson likes nothing better than to catch someone out with one of his practical jokes and he caught a lot of people out with that electric fence of his.

"I went down to collect a donkey from the farm about fifteen years ago shortly after the fence had been put up and I bumped into him . "Ah, the very man I'm looking for," he said. There's a fence in the backfield I'd like you to take a look at, Jimmy It's

122

the best fence in all of Ireland without exception for keeping animals in. I'd like your opinion on it."

We went round to the field and I laughed and laughed when I saw the fence Swinson was boasting about. It was as miserable a looking a fence as I'd ever seen. It had one single strand of wire that hardly came up to my thigh and Swinson setting great store by it to keep his animals in.

"Now, Mr Swinson, I don't mean to criticise," I said, "but that fence wouldn't hold a two year old baby let alone a two year old heifer."

"Jimmy, you're a doubting Thomas," Swinson said with a grin the size of Slievegart Bay.

I wondered why he looked so pleased with himself but I soon found out.

"That fence of mine would hold in ten bulls without any bother," he said. "And I'm prepared to bet on it."

"I'm not a betting man. I'd never bet in my life but if I did bet I'd put a lot of money up against you now, Mr Swinson," I said. "I thought he had taken leave of his senses saying that wire would contain ten bulls."

I felt like butting in and trying to get Jimmy to hurry up until I glanced at Sara and saw the look on her face. She was enthralled by Jimmy's story. It was probably the most talking he had ever done in one sitting since their courting days and, after all, she had waited over half a century to hear his story.

"There's no way that fence would hold in one bull, Mr Swinson, never mind ten, no way at all. You must have taken leave of your senses. I told him. To tell you the truth, Doctor, I was feeling badly out of sorts and impatient with it. I was in no mood for Swinson's jokes. The butterflies in my chest had been going on for two days nonstop. I hadn't slept a wink in twenty-four hours even with all the gate jumping and water ducking in the world and I was starting to feel weak."

"Go on, then, Jimmy," Mr Swinson said to me. "Grab the wire and see if you can break it and here's ten pounds that says you can't, even if you don't want to bet against me."

"I was fired up by then with vexation and anger at his teasing and the butterflies and I spat on my hands to give me a better grip. That seemed to amuse Swinson no end and that made me crosser and more determined than ever to show him up. I grabbed the wire with both hands, determined to break it and got the surprise of my life. An awful pain went right through me. Some of those electric fences were far too heavily charged when they first came out. I was thrown backwards as if I'd been picked up and flung down by a giant. I landed heavily on the flat of my back. I didn't know what had happened. I thought I'd maybe been struck by lightning. I was a hardy man then and jumped straight back up and grabbed that wire again and I was put on my back for a second time.

"Swinson was laughing so much he had gone red in the face. I thought he was going to die laughing from a heart attack.

"Jimmy," he said "that was the best value for money I've ever had especially when you got up like a jack in the box and took a second electric shock for the price of one. That was priceless. I'll give you the tenner if you go over and do it again."

"I was tempted to run over and punch him on the nose when I noticed a strange thing. The butterflies had completely gone and I felt back to my normal self in an instant. There must have been something in that electric shock that put those butterflies away. In a second, I'd gone from feeling weak and badly off form to being relieved and delighted and as strong as an ox again."

As I listened to Jimmy, I began to see everything falling into place and to understand why his strange antics had helped him over all those years. Jimmy had paroxysmal supraventricular tachycardia. That is a heart condition which can come on at any age but most frequently in the teens for reasons not entirely known.

The heart starts to race for no apparent reason and it can race for anything from several seconds to several days. It gives the butterfly feeling in the chest that Jimmy had described. That explained why jumping off the gate worked and made him feel right. It jolted his heart and sent it back to its normal rhythm. Putting his head under water made him hold his breath which increased the pressure on his neck and face. That increased the pressure on small organs called the carotoid sinuses which are found inside the carotid arteries, the biggest arteries in the neck. Increased pressure on the carotid sinuses slows the heart down.

I remembered my old, eccentric cardiology teacher in Dublin talking about paroxysmal supra ventricular tachycardia (SVT).

"Now lads and lassies," Dr Brennan would say, "we're dealing with one of the commonest causes of pathological fast hearts in the world so you'd better listen carefully. This is bread and butter medicine and this is where you'll make yourselves a few dollars if you do any private medicine or if you ever emigrate to the U.S. of A. The diagnosis is made by listening to the patient or, as the famous Sir William Osler, one of the founding fathers of modern Medicine said, 'listen to the patient, he's telling you the diagnosis.' The patient will tell you ninety nine times out of one hundred that he has the feeling of butterflies in his chest which starts suddenly and stops suddenly. The heart races along, at a regular rate of 140 beats per minute. If it lasts for longer than twenty minutes, the patient will usually go off and pass a fair volume of water.

You can slow the heart down in most cases by rubbing the carotid sinus or increasing the pressure on it by getting the patient to hold his breath and force the breath against the throat.

"If those simple procedures don't work then it's time for the jungle juice, beta blockers are the drug of choice, the flavour of the month. If they don't work then it's down to the electrics, shock them twice, once with the cardio converter and the second time with your big fat fee."

Dr Brennan's often repeated manta made a lot of sense as far as Jimmy was concerned.

"So what do you think of all of that for a story, Doctor?" Jimmy ended up by saying. "Am I as mad as people say or is there method in my madness?"

"I think I need to examine you, Mr Scullion. That's what I think. Have you any of those butterflies at the moment?"

"I have them a little," he said, "but nothing serious. I think all the excitement of talking about myself for so long brought them on. I'm not used to that woman staring at me like that either. It makes me nervous," and he nodded towards Sara who was looking at him with a glow on her cheeks and affection in her eyes. She was touched by how much Jimmy had endured over the years without ever complaining.

"In a way, it's good, you have the butterflies no matter what the cause and I think it's love myself on this occasion," I said taking the stethoscope out of my bag and smiling at Sara, "because hopefully I can make a diagnosis and once you've made a diagnosis, you can treat the condition."

I applied the stethoscope to Jimmy's chest and there it was, the heart flying along at 140 beats a minute. I explained to Jimmy and Sara as best I could what was wrong with him and why jumping off gates and ducking his head in buckets of water had helped him over the years.

"I know you don't like hospitals and doctors or tablets but there is treatment nowadays for this sort of condition," I said. "If you prefer, you can continue to jump off pillars and gates until you break your leg or you can try these pills."

Jimmy smiled, "I think my jumping days are almost over. I'll let Sara do the jumping from now on and I'll take the tablets."

I wrote him out a prescription for Beta blockers and told him if they didn't work (and it would have been unusual if they didn't) there were electric shock techniques for stabilising the heart. "And they're considerably more refined and less painful than Mr Swinson's electric fence,"

Jimmy laughed. He went with me to the end of the lane and thanked me as he shook my hand. I called Bonnie who had been waiting patiently in the yard and set off down the hilly slopes to Slievegart.

I felt elated at making such a diagnosis without the benefit of an electrocardiogram and treating such a debilitating condition so quickly. It made me feel like a real doctor. I began to whistle as I drove home and that started Bonnie howling. We must have looked a couple of idiots, me whistling happily and Bonnie sitting up tall beside me, nose pointed in the air, yelping happily out of the Landrover window.

We rounded a curve in the road and the Atlantic Ocean and the wonderful coastline came into view. Maybe this doctoring business wasn't so bad after all.

Blind Man's Bluff

"Would you just sign that little form for me there, Dr Griffin, like a good man, if you'd be so kind and I'll be on my way and leave you in peace to see the rest of your patients in that packed waiting room," Alfie Reid said as he pushed a grubby, much folded form across the desk. All I could see under Alfie's dirty thumb was a box with Doctor's Signature written beside it.

"What is it Alfie?" I asked, immediately suspicious. I didn't trust Alfie. There was something a bit shifty about him. I couldn't put my finger on it but every time he came to the surgery for his three weekly injection of vitamins, I got the same feeling, a likeable enough old man but not to be entirely trusted.

"Oh it's only a little form of no consequence, Doctor. If you'll just be so good as to sign it and let me give you the peace you deserve after all the hard work you've been doing this morning in Slievegart."

There was an unctuousness to his flattery that just didn't ring true. It was in keeping with his appearance. Hilda had once described him as a long string of misery from the day and hour he'd been born.

Alfie was seventy years old and had a thirty year history of diabetes and vitamin B12 deficiency. Over the years his sight had deteriorated until he had been registered blind two years previously.

I had my suspicions about how blind he really was. He wore dark glasses and was very reluctant to remove them for any kind of examination. The way he looked straight at me when he spoke wasn't the way that most blind people did. Alfie carried a white cane but didn't seem to need it except when he flicked it at a dog or a child who got in his way.

He reminded me of a man I had seen at a point-to-point meeting when I was a boy. That blind man had sat begging in a gap between two fields where everyone passed by and had done very well for himself. When the meeting was over and everyone had gone home except for a few of us boys who had stayed on for a bit of horse play, I saw the man get up and glance round. When he saw he was alone, he took off his dark glasses and put them in his pocket and threw his white stick into a bag with all his takings. I'm not saying Alfie was as untrustworthy as that but there was something about him that reminded me of the beggar. I knew he was getting himself one or two extra allowances since he had registered blind.

I picked the form up that Alfie had inched across the table and unfolded it. Small pieces of dirt and a few crumbs fell out of the folds. The form must have been in his pocket for weeks, probably waiting for an opportunity like this when I was under pressure and would sign nearly anything.

"I'll just have a look at this form, Alfie, if you don't mind," I said in my being friendly but not really liking the situation voice.

"Ah there's no need to bother yourself looking at it at all. It's hardly worth the trouble you doing that Doctor. If you'll just sign there," and he pointed to the bottom of the grubby form. "I'll be on my way and let you settle down. I expect you've got a lot to do dealing with the sick and it'll speed up your cup of tea and you need it after a hard morning's surgery."

Alfie had a way of making it sound as though he was getting me to sign the form for my benefit and not his.

"I'll just have a read of the form anyway, if you don't mind."

There was no way I was going to sign any form, and particularly one for Alfie, without reading it first. Professor WJPR Soames, our Professor of Medicine in Dublin words echoed in my ear. He had a number of epigrams and sayings he used to repeat frequently in his rich, plummy voice.

"Ladies and Gentlemen, might I remind you that your name is (and he always emphasised the word is) your reputation. Never put your name to anything you're not prepared to stand by and are prepared to stand by in court if the situation arises."

He had repeated this so often I would hardly sign for a recorded delivery until I'd read all the details.

"Ah, Doctor, there's no need at all to do that. Don't trouble yourself reading that old form and the dirt of it too destroying your lovely clean desk and you being such a busy man...."

Was I right or did Alfie sound a little anxious?

"It's no trouble at all, Alfie, in fact it's a pleasure for me to be given the opportunity to help a man like yourself," I said as I opened out the form and read the words, DRIVING LICENCE.

"Driving licence?" I exclaimed in astonishment. "Driving licence, Alfie? What on earth do you need a driving licence for and you registered blind?"

"Ah, Ah, Ah, I must have brought along the wrong form," Alfie mumbled. "I meant to bring the form along for my gun .... no, I mean my dog licence."

I didn't believe a word he said.

"You don't need a doctor's signature for a dog licence," I said.

"Don't you now? Isn't it all confusing the way they keep changing the rules. I could have sworn the Gardai told me I needed my dog licence signed by a doctor."

"But you haven't got a dog, Alfie."

"No, no and so I haven't but I was thinking of getting one. They say a dog for the blind is just the thing I need and I'll go now straight away and look into it, if I could just take my little form with me." He leaned forward and tried to grab the form. I was too quick for him as I pulled it out of his reach. "Not a bad reaction for a blind man " I thought.

"Maybe it was the gun licence you had in mind for me to sign, Alfie?"

"Ah, Doctor, now you must be joking, What would a man like me be doing with a gun licence? That's a hoot that is. You've a sense of humour you have, Doc, the way you're pulling my leg."

I said nothing. One of his neighbours had told me the previous week he had seen Alfie out in his back garden trying to shoot a fox that had killed his chickens and, for a man with difficulty seeing, he had been shooting pretty accurately.

When I remained silent, Alfie started to blabber.

"Maybe it wasn't the gun or the dog licence at all, Doctor. Maybe I'm not making much sense because my blood sugar has gone too low, you see, what with me being a diabetic and hypoglycaemic at times. Do you think that would be the cause of all this confusion and me talking nonsense and asking you to sign a car and a gun licence, sure nobody normal would do that?" and Alfie started flopping about as if was on the verge of passing out.

"How did you get up here, Alfie?" I asked ignoring his antics.

"I'm too confused now to remember," he said putting his hand across his forehead as if he was about to faint.

"Well try and remember, Alfie, or I'll maybe have to ask the Gardai to help you jog your memory," I said sternly.

"Sure it's not important how I got here as long as I'm here for my injection now, is it?"

I was determined to pin Alfie down.

"Now tell me Alfie, in your own words how did you get here today. Was it in your own car?"

"It was in my sister's car. This weakness I have in my head is coming back. My blood sugar must be unmeasurable by now."

"And did your sister drive it?" I asked.

I knew the answer to that question and Alfie knew that I knew. His sister Gertrude had taken a small stroke soon after I had arrived in Slievegart and I had attended her. She'd had to relinquish her driving licence because of it.

"Well, not exactly."

"Not exactly, Alfie? What does that mean. You either drive a car or you don't. You can't not exactly drive a car. Did Gertrude drive the car here today because as far as I'm concerned she gave up her driving licence? The Gardai would be very interested to hear about that."

"Maybe it would be best if I went out and spoke to Gertrude and let her explain."

"Would it now, Alfie?"

Alfie gave a deep sigh. He knew the game was up.

"I drove it," he said.

"You drove it," I said in astonishment.

I knew Alfie was a bit of a rogue and I knew he wasn't as blind as he pretended to be but he did have extremely limited vision. I had expected him to say he had got a young lad of fourteen or fifteen who hadn't got a licence to drive a car but knew how to drive a tractor to drive him to the surgery.

"Yes Doctor, I drove here."

Now that he had been found out, there was a note of defiance, almost pride, in his voice.

"And how did you manage to do that when you're registered blind?"

"Oh, I managed well enough, Doctor. Gertrude has the vision though she has had a bit of a stroke and can't drive herself. She directs me. She's sort of my co-pilot."

"Gertrude directs you?"

Now that did surprise me. Gertrude was the exact opposite of Alfie. She was a small, prim and proper woman who was always dressed immaculately. She had been a teacher in a small private school in England and was quite the school ma'am. She did everything by the book and was meticulously honest. When she retired, she came back to Kerry and settled in with Alfie. Neither of them had ever married and, despite their differences in personality, they seemed to get on well together.

"Aye, Gertrude gives me the instructions and I do the driving end of things."

"What sort of instructions does Gertrude give you?"

"Well, she backs me on to the road and tells me if I'm too near the hedge or if a car is coming. We only go out at quiet times when there's not much traffic about, early in the morning or late on in the afternoon. She tells me to pull in if she sees another car coming or if I'm driving in the middle of the road or too near the ditch, that sort of thing. It's more for getting to the shops and coming up here and going to the Chapel for Mass on a

Sunday and, for the life of us, you wouldn't want us to miss Mass on a Sunday now, would you, Dr Griffin?"

I almost began to feel sorry for him but I had to be ruthless. I had to think of other road users.

"I'm sorry, Alfie, I can't possibly sign your form. It wouldn't be right. I can arrange for Hilda to call every three weeks to give you your injection at home. That will save you having to come up here. You'll have to get Molloy's mobile shop to call with you for your groceries and I'm sure Father McKinney will give you a dispensation from going to Mass."

"Right you are then," Alfie said as he stood up. "If that's the way it has to be then that's the way it has to be. If you'd be so good as to get someone to phone Paddy O'Brien's taxi, I'll get myself and Gertrude a lift home and send someone up to bring the car home later."

Two or three weeks later, Hilda came into the surgery. She was a little breathless.

"You'll never guess who I saw riding a motor bike along the back road to Slievegart this morning," she said, "and on the wrong side of the road too."

"Don't tell me it was Alfie Reid," I said.

"The very man, and guess who was riding pillion."

"McGinty's goat."

"No, don't be silly James, guess again."

"The Queen of Belgium."

"No. Has Belgium got a Queen? Guess again."

"Gertrude Gwendoline Mary Josephine Reid."

"Herself exactly, good old Gerty sitting on the back of that 50cc motorbike like she was a Hells Angel out cruising for trouble. I never thought she had it in her or that I'd live to see a blind man ride a motor bike and his sister with a stroke behind him giving directions and not a helmet between them."

"To tell you the truth Hilda, I never did either," was all I could say. And I always thought the young were meant to be the foolish ones. At least, that was what Professor Soames used to tell us in his more lucid moments.

Darby and Joans

I opened the waiting room door one sunny morning and my heart sank. It wasn't because the surgery was full of nervous four year olds waiting for their vaccinations and the fact I hated giving children injections, especially the sort that clung to their mothers like limpets. It was because of the couple that were sitting in the middle of the children with grim expressions on their faces. The McFaddens were the two biggest moaners I had ever met in my medical career. Their miserable faces were enough to put anyone off ever wanting to become a doctor.

Frog face Freddie and Dilly Dally Sally, as they were known in the village, were in their sixties. You never saw one without the other.

Fred was tall, thin and miserable looking. He wore a cloth cap whatever the weather and had a permanent runny nose that he wiped with the sleeve of his coat. Fred had a perpetual look of anxiety on his face. He never smiled. There was only one subject in the world that seemed to interest him and that was the state of his health or lack of it. He believed he was the sickest and most unfortunate man in Ireland. Maybe he was when you considered that he was married to Sally, who complained more than he did if that was possible.

Sally was short and plump. She invariably wore a grubby overcoat and a squashed straw hat that looked like an upturned bowl on her head. Her lips were plastered with lipstick and her eyes lined with mascara. That, combined with generous daubings of rouge on both cheeks, gave her the appearance of a circus clown, a grotesque and very unfunny clown.

The two of them were always bickering though poor Fred always seemed to end up the loser. No matter where she was or whose company she was in, if Fred annoyed Sally and that wasn't a difficult thing to do, she exploded and screamed at him with such venom it frightened anyone who happened to be standing nearby. It certainly frightened mild mannered Fred.

Sally and Fred had no children or pets. They didn't believe in throwing anything away and their house was full of clutter. Neither of them had worked within living memory. They came to the surgery at least twice a week and took up forty minutes each time.

I found their visits tedious in the extreme - forty minutes of unrelenting, mindless grumbling. Hilda told me they were the bane of Dr Robert's life. He couldn't get rid of them either in anything under thirty minutes and that consoled me.

Nothing was too trivial to escape their attention and I mean nothing. Fred had phoned me in an absolute panic at seven o'clock that particular morning because he had passed urine twice during the night instead of his usual once.

"What do you think is wrong with me?" he had asked in near panic. "Do you think I've cancer of the prostrate gland?"

"Mr McFadden," I mumbled waking from a deep sleep, "you definitely do not have cancer of the prostrate gland."

I didn't feel like pointing out that the gland was the prostate and not the prostrate. Prostrate was what I had been before I got his daft call.

"Then why has this dreadful thing happened to me?"

"For goodness sake," I felt like saying, "pull yourself together. You call passing water twice during the night dreadful. Try having cancer or multiple sclerosis or motor neuron disease and then you'll really know what dreadful is." It would have been pointless taking that approach with him. He wouldn't have known what I was talking about. To him, his symptoms were more important than any calamity in the world, I knew he would pester Hilda and me about it for weeks if I couldn't come up with a good answer to why he had urinated twice instead of the customary once.

"Did you drink any more tea than usual yesterday, Mr McFadden?" I asked.

"Oh no," he said. He seemed quite shocked at the suggestion. "I am a man of habit. I never change my routine. I take three mugs of tea a day and the last one is at ten o'clock at night with half a slice of bread and a light touch of marmite on it before I go to bed."

"It was very warm yesterday. You wouldn't have drunk a drop more water than usual?"

"Oh no, no, no." He was alarmed I might think for a second that he would vary his routine under any circumstances.

"You didn't even take a small glass of water in all the heat of the day?"

"No, no doctor, I don't trust the water from the tap."

"You didn't have a beer?"

"I never drink doctor. It's bad for my health and it makes me belch like a bullock." I didn't like the sound of that.

"Could you have maybe taken an extra water tablet for the fluid on your legs I gave you last week?" I nearly added for the imaginary fluid.

I was getting desperate. It's much harder dealing with people who think they are sick than dealing with people who are sick,

"Oh no doctor, I did exactly as you told me when you gave me them tablets last Tuesday, one a day and one a day only."

"For goodness sake," I thought crossly, "you silly methodical clown. Did it ever enter your head to do anything spontaneous? In all of your sixty two years, did you ever think of seizing life by the scruff of its neck and enjoying yourself?"

I kept my thoughts to myself with difficulty. I tried desperately to think of a plausible answer to this most trivial of problems that would stop him from pestering me for the next two or three weeks. Nothing came to mind, absolutely nothing. The knock on effects of Fred's anxiety was unthinkable if I didn't come up with something. My silence was unnerving Fred. I could hear him breathing anxiously on the other end of the phone.

"You're not trying to hide something from me Dr Griffin, are you? You don't think it's anything serious do you?" His voice was very tense.

"No Fred, I don't." I was almost tempted to tell him I'd got up myself twice the previous night to pass water after I'd had a bottle of beer and a pint of tea to myself. I knew that would be of no interest or consolation to him. Professor W.J.P.R. Soames would never have approved of that approach anyway. "Never ever reveal anything of a personal nature to a patient or encourage familiarity which is detrimental to the doctor / patient relationship," he used to say. I was going to have to keep my little secret to myself.

Fred persisted. "You don't sound too sure about my problem, if you don't mind me saying so, doctor," he said.

"I'm surer than sure about your problem Fred. It's not serious." I said.

"Not serious doctor. Are you sure you're sure it's not serious?"

"I'm totally and absolutely and utterly sure that passing urine twice in the middle of the night on one occasion is not serious, Fred."

There was a pause of several seconds while Fred reflected on that before he continued.

"Maybe I should come in," he said.

"Come in Fred?" What was he talking about? What did he mean? Was he outside on top of his henhouse waiting for my permission to come in?

"Yes. Come in and see you, doctor."

"Come in and see me Fred? No, I don't think that's necessary. That's not necessary at all."

"But I really think I should."

I realised there was no point arguing with him once he had his mind made up.

"And when were you thinking of coming in?"

"Right now doctor, right this very minute to get this thing sorted out."

I exclaimed in alarm. "Oh no, oh no Fred, I don't think so. Not at this time in the morning. This is something that can wait until the morning surgery and a lot longer than that, believe me."

"But I think it's serious."

"I know you think it's serious Fred but I'm telling you with one hundred percent certainly, it's not serious."

Fred wasn't listening.

"I need to get to the bottom of this and get some answers or this is going to get a grip of me. I'm getting myself into a state about it and you know what I'm like when I get into a state."

"Fred," I said sternly, "there's absolutely no need for you to come in, no need at all. You're not in a state about it or anywhere near a state. Do you think you could possibly be over reacting a little?"

"No doctor, I don't, not at all. It's worrying when things like this happen out of the blue and, begging your pardon, your doctor can't explain why." He hesitated before continuing. "Do you think I should maybe give Dr O'Flathertie a call about my problem and see what he thinks. I'm not trying to put you down in any way Dr Griffin, but Dr O'Flathertie has years of experience behind him and he might be able to give me some answers. If I don't get some answers, I'll fret and when I fret it makes everything ten times worse so I hope you wouldn't mind if I give him a call."

"No, no, no, I wouldn't mind in the least," I told him trying to hide my enthusiasm for Fred's latest idea. "Nothing would give me greater pleasure than for you to call Dr O'Flathertie. You're entitled to a second opinion and Dr O'Flathertie will certainly give you that."

My only regret was I couldn't be a fly on the wall in the O'Flathertie's bedroom when that call came through.

"Do you think Dr O'Flathertie would mind?" he asked.

I couldn't bring myself to tell him I thought Dr O'Flathertie would be delighted. I knew I would only start laughing if I did.

"Why should he mind, Fred. He's a doctor and he's there to help people. That's his job."

"Are you sure he wouldn't mind?"

"What makes you think he would?"

"I know Dr O'Flathertie can be a bit cross and impatient sometimes. That's why Sally and me left his practice twenty odd years ago. He told Sally when she went to see him about her bunions one Sunday morning that there was nothing wrong with her that a good boot up her back end wouldn't cure and that I was to buy myself a good pair of industrial boots with steel caps on Monday morning and give her a fair hard booting up and down the garden every time she complained."

"That was an interesting concept," I said as I tried to stop myself laughing at the picture of the lanky Fred with his cap half over his eyes chasing Sally up and down the garden trying to plant his boot on her retreating figure. "And how did Sally feel about that advice?"

"She told him that he was a good for nothing, ignorant man who wasn't fit to be dealing with animals let alone human beings."

I was intrigued with Dr O'Flathertie's eccentric behaviour and unorthodox advice. Hardly a day went by without someone telling me of something extraordinary he had said or done. When they told me they were either livid with anger or choked with laughter, I sometimes thought it was a wonder that Dr O'Flathertie had any patients at all.

"And what did Dr O'Flathertie say when Sally said that to him?" I asked.

"He said that if she wasn't out of his surgery in ten seconds flat, he wouldn't be responsible for his actions."

"So Sally left?"

"She did indeed. Sally wasn't the better of it for a month. She said she'd rather die than let that man come within a hundred yards of her so I don't know if she'd be too pleased if I phone him about my waterworks. I suppose I better ask her. Do you think I should, doctor?" and he put the phone down before I could answer. I held on for two minutes and was about to put the phone down when I heard him hurrying back.

"No, sorry, doctor, that's not on at all," he said. "Not on at all, at all, at all. That's a complete non starter. Sally's in a right state already with me even mentioning that man's name."

"Is she now, Fred?" I was beginning to feel in a bit of a state myself with all the time I had wasted.

"So will I come and see you?"

"Yes, Fred but not now. Come to the morning surgery. 10a.m. sharp."

"Do you think I'll be alright till then?"

"You'll be as safe as houses until then. Goodbye now," I said and slammed the phone down before he could think of something else to worry about. I gasped for air for several minutes. Even though there was something likeable about Fred, he still was the most mind-numbing, tedious man I had ever spoken to. I couldn't get back to sleep after that so I went down and made myself a pot of coffee. I drank it out on the lawn and watched the trawlers coming back from their night's fishing. As usual, Charlie O'Shea's dirty old black trawler lagged behind all the others. Phil Ban lead the fleet in, in his sleek Sancta Maria and I thought as I watched them that I would have to try and get a trip out on one of these boats, when a storm threatened so that I could really try out my sea legs.

Sitting back and watching the beauty of the scene in front of me filled me with a feeling of peace until I went in and opened the surgery door at ten o'clock. Fred and Sally stood up straight away to be seen even though there were about ten people in the waiting room in front of them. As far as they were concerned, there was nobody there with problems as important as theirs.

The young mothers looked up in surprise as the elderly couple darted towards my office. They didn't protest. They were enjoying chatting to each other and the children were happy enough. It wouldn't have been possible to stop Sally in any case, not when she was in one of her determined moods. She had told me the previous week she could hardly walk her own length on account of her bad leg. That bad leg was now propelling her across the waiting room like a piston pump. They rushed into the surgery and sat down. Sally immediately started into a tirade.

"What's this you phoning Dr O'Flathertie about me, Dr Griffin. It's none of his business knowing what I'm doing. He's an ignorant old..."

"Hold on a minute, Mrs McFadden," I said. "What are you talking about? I never said anything about phoning Dr O'Flathertie about you. Fred said he was going to phone...."

"It was you then, you little liar and not the doctor," Sally roared. "I should have known. I'll deal with you later my Boyo."

Sally was not a woman to cross. I glanced at Fred. He looked like a dog who had just been kicked and was waiting for the next blow to land.

"Now doctor," Sally's voice had reverted to her usual whine. "What about me then?"

"What about you?" I asked in surprise. "I saw you two days ago, Mrs McFadden and everything was fine then. Your blood pressure and everything was normal."

"Two days ago was two days. A lot can happen in two days. Fred can have his say when I've had mine. There's nothing wrong with him anyway. He's always going on about himself. Now, what's my blood pressure like doctor? It needs to be checked again after all the shock I've been through with that scamp O'Flathertie, about to poke his big nose into my affairs"

She put her fat arm out to have the blood pressure cuff put on.

"But you had your blood pressure taken two days ago, Mrs McFadden, and it was perfect then," I protested.

"As I said a lot can happen in two days. That lightness is back in my head and you know what that can mean."

It was pointless arguing with her. I measured her blood pressure to save time. It was normal.

"And what about the ticker?"

I put the stethoscope against her chest and listened.

"Couldn't be better," I said.

"And the lungs? Are they O.K.?"

141

"Fine," I said as I brushed the stethoscope lightly across her back.

"And my pulse? Is that normal?"

"It's extra good," I said as I gave it a quick check.

"So everything's in order then, Dr Griffin?"

"Yes, everything is working fine. You'll live to be a hundred if not more." I couldn't believe my luck that I had finished with Sally so quickly.

"Oh, I don't know about that. I like a wee check up now and again. Isn't it better to be sure than sorry? You can't be too careful nowadays."

"Now about Fred," I said grimacing at her platitudes.

"Hold on there a minute, Dr Griffin," Sally interrupted. "You haven't finished with me yet. I'm only just starting. I've got my list of complaints here" and she pulled out a piece of crumpled paper and began to unfold it. "You young doctors are too keen to get finished up early and put your feet up and enjoy yourselves, not like the old time doctors who had time for their patients and really looked after them. It's a nice little earner being a doctor I can tell you. I would have been one myself only I didn't have the health to study."

I gritted my teeth. I had heard this particular lecture before, many times. It particularly irked me with Sally who had never done a day's work in her life.

Hilda had been at school with her and she told me that Sally had been a big, fat, lazy lump of a girl even then.

"Now here we are," she said unruffling the piece of paper, "my wee list."

I could see she had at least seven complaints written down. "Now let's go through these one at a time," and she put her reading glasses on.

"Now," she said, "why am I so breathless if my heart and lungs are so good?"

I was beginning to feel annoyed at being taken advantage of by this woman and letting her jump the queue all for the sake of peace. I should have insisted on seeing Fred first and not waste all this time with Sally when I had a roomful of children waiting to be vaccinated. I felt like telling her bluntly why she was breathless. It was because she was five stone overweight and hadn't taken any meaningful exercise in the whole of her life. She had never done anything more strenuous than suck a bottle when she had been a baby. I knew a reply like that would only delay matters and send Sally into a fury and she would become abusive. I answered her questions as quickly as I could while she laboriously read them out. This went on for fifteen minutes, I thought she had finished when she announced she had a new symptom since I saw her last which she had saved to the end.

I groaned inwardly. This was worse than usual and I still had Fred to deal with. Sally droned on oblivious to my angst,

"I want to get to the bottom of this complaint from the word go," she stated.

"Well, what is the complaint?" I had trouble stopping myself snapping at her.

"Total body pain," she said.

"Total body pain?" That was a new one on me.

"Yes, there isn't a part of my body that isn't aching and hurting. Even my teeth are hurting."

"Maybe you should see a dentist," I said clutching at straws.

"See a dentist! Why would I want to see a dentist?"

"You said your teeth hurt......"

"Along with all the rest of me. Every living part of me is sore. It's not a dentist I need to see, it's a specialist in total body pain I need to see."

I sighed. If only they existed, my life would have been so much easier.

"Unfortunately," I said, "I've never heard of specialists in total body pain, Mrs McFadden. If I had I would certainly refer you and Fred to one immediately."

I saw Fred's face lighten at the mention of his name associated with something medical. Fred really did need to get a life.

"Why aren't there specialists in total body pain when so many people are suffering from it?" Sally demanded angrily. "Mrs McVey told me only last week she has the exact same complaint as me and her doctor is sending her to a specialist about it."

I sensed Sally was suggesting Mrs McVey's doctor was far superior and more caring than me and more up to date too. He knew all about total body pain specialists.

"Mrs McFadden, if you could find out the name of that specialist and where he works, I'll be only too happy to refer you to him."

"How can I do that with me in the pain I'm in. It's your job to know about those things and if you don't know how do you expect an old woman in pain like me to find out. The cheek of you suggesting me, chase after that Biddy McVey one to see whose she's attending. Who do you think I am?" Sally sat there like an enraged cockerel.

It was typical of her, indeed of most moaners. They are not prepared to lift a finger to help themselves but expect everyone else to be at their beck and call.

I'm normally a peaceful man but I'd had enough of Sally and her self centred, bad mannered whinging. Deep down I have a Dr O'Flahertie type gene and I could feel the first inklings of it stirring inside me.

"Mrs McFadden," I said, "I don't think it's unreasonable to ask you to find out the name of Mrs McVey's specialist if you want to be referred to him......."

"I have no notion of finding out. That's your job. The insolence of you suggesting I chase after that McVey woman and let her know my business." Sally was shouting now in her hectoring 'nobody's going to tell me what to do' tone.

"If you're not prepared to help yourself at all, Mrs McFadden," I retorted "then this consultation is now over."

"What do you mean this consultation is over," she snorted in angry astonishment. She couldn't have been more surprised if I'd suddenly jumped on top of my desk and started to tap dance.

"Don't you tell me this consultation is over you cheeky young upstart, you jumped up excuse for a doctor. This consultation is over when I say it is over and not one second before."

Sally really was working herself up now. She was thumping my desk with her fist and had thrust her face so far forward it was only a matter of inches away from mine. She was screaming and her normally pale face had turned a beetroot red. I could see the veins in her neck bulging out like cords.

"If she doesn't calm herself down," I thought, "she's going to take a heart attack or a stroke."

I didn't speak. I couldn't think of anything to say. Somehow I had to get her to calm down before she collapsed and died in front of me. I knew there was no way she would ever admit to being wrong. I would have to back down. I didn't want Sally to die in my surgery and have that on my conscience.

"Look, Mrs McFadden...."

"Don't you Mrs McFadden me you ignorant young man. Dr Roberts never spoke to me like that in his entire life." Sally had reverted to her angry, self pitying, 'I've been hard done by' voice.

She wasn't making things easy for me. My thoughts went to Dr O'Flatherie. He would have been as pleased as punch with himself for putting Sally in her place. He wouldn't have been one bit worried about her taking a stroke.

We sat staring at each other. I was resigned to the fact this was going to take the best part of the morning to resolve. Professor W.J.P.R. Soames would have settled this scene much more professionally, I thought of my old tutor. I could picture him leaning across his desk in his blue pin striped suit, his glasses on the end of his nose and the tips of his fingers of both hands together in the shape of a tent as he looked directly into Sally's eyes.

"That will do Mrs McFadden. That is quite enough" He would have said long, long ago. "My rule is never to deal with more than two complaints at one consultation. I'm going to arrange for a colleague of mine to see you. He will write to you with an appointment in the next two or three days."

He would have ignored all Sally's protests and questions as he helped her to her feet and guided or pulled her, if necessary, to the door.

"In the meantime, I suggest you take plenty of rest and fresh air, Mrs McFadden," and the door would have been closed firmly behind her before she knew where she was.

My gloomy thoughts were interrupted by a persistent knocking on the door. I dragged myself to my feet to answer it. It was Hilda. I was never more pleased to see anyone. She winked at me.

"I need to have a word with you in private immediately," she announced. "It's about an urgent call you need to attend to," she said in a voice loud enough for Sally and Fred to hear.

"Where is it to, Hilda?"

"If you follow me, I'll give you the details."

I followed her next door into the kitchen. She immediately handed me a cup of coffee and a plate of biscuits.

"You'll probably need these after that carry on, James," she said sympathetically. "I heard all that shouting in there when I was having a chat with the nippers and their mothers in the waiting room. You should have seen their faces when Sally started roaring. It was like a pantomime. The children all ran back to their mothers in a fright.

Now, if you go back in there, Sally is going to waste your whole morning with her histrionics. The best thing would be for me to go in and settle her down and send her on her way. I know how to handle her. You can go off and see Eddie Muldoon. He'll cheer you up if anyone can and to think old Eddie nearly married Sally. I don't think he'd be so jolly today if he had. I was going to ask you to see him tomorrow but, in the circumstances, today might be more appropriate."

"Hilda, I really appreciate you trying to bail me out and get me away from that McFadden woman, I really do but I have all those pre-school vaccinations to do after I've sorted Sally and Fred out."

"Oh don't be ridiculous, James. You're in no state to deal with those children. I'll give them their injections. I enjoy seeing them anyway and hearing how they're growing up. It'll be a pleasure for me. Now, away with you."

I thanked Hilda profusely as I went out to the Landrover. I was so relieved to be leaving Sally behind. I would happily have spread cow manure on a farm all day rather than face her again. Hilda had even put Bonnie into the passenger seat. She knew the dog would calm me down and take my mind off the McFaddens. The memory of Hilda's kindness remained with me all my life and influenced my own approach to people in trouble and at the end of their tether.

I told Hilda as I clambered into the Landrover that Fred would probably give her an earful about his urinary problems"

"Ah, don't you be worrying about that, James," she said. "I'll tell him you looked it up in a big medical book and that urinating twice in a night can be a very healthy sign for a man of his age. It's the body ridding itself of toxins."

Sally didn't come back to the surgery for a month, the longest break ever. Fred accepted Hilda's explanation about it being beneficial to urinate twice at night but when it happened again two weeks later, he began to worry where all the toxins were coming from. The only way I could stop him worrying was to send him to a kidney specialist. Unfortunately I never did find out the name of that total body pain specialist that Sally so urgently needed.

The String Vest

"Tom Slattery's pig has more manners than that ingnoramus," was how Dr O'Flathertie described Billy Harper. I thought that was a bit harsh but when I came to know Billy better, I understood Dr O'Flathertie's reasoning.

I was feeling elated after finishing a weekend call one bright Monday morning. I decided to start the surgery early so I could finish early and get away down to the sea but when I opened the surgery door, my heart sank. The room was packed. It was standing room only and Billy was there towering over everyone. He was leaning against a wall smoking a cigarette despite a no smoking sign right in front of his eyes. A couple of elderly patients who suffered from asthma had gone outside to get away from the fog of smoke. It sounded as if they were trying to cough up their lungs.

Billy wasn't bothered in the slightest as he blew clouds of thick smoke into the air. I asked him to put his cigarette out. He completely ignored me and took a deep drag before blowing a long stream of smoke in my direction. I walked over to him and insisted he put his cigarette out immediately. He gave me an angry look and slowly nipped the butt between two nicotine stained fingers. He put the smouldering cigarette end behind one of his ears. I hoped he would burn himself but he didn't.

"Dr O'Flatherite is right," I thought, "Billy is one ignorant man."

When I called the first patient in, Billy made a move to come in pushing the other patients to one side even though he had been the last to arrive. Hilda had warned me about his queue jumping tactics.

"I'm sorry, Mr Harper," I said, "but Eugene is first on the list," and I indicated a timid lad of sixteen who seemed terrified of Billy.

Eugene sprang to his feet like a frightened rabbit and bolted into my room. Billy objected.

"What are you seeing him first for. There's nothing wrong with that young git and I'm in a hurry. I was here before him anyway."

"I'm sure you're in a hurry," I thought to myself, "in a hurry to get down to Muldoon's lounge bar for a feed of drink."

"I'm sorry, Mr Harper. According to Nurse Armstrong (Hilda) Eugene was here first. She took everyone's names as they arrived. If you're in a hurry, I suggest you come back when you're under less pressure. As it is, there are eleven people in front of you. It will take me a long time to see them all, an hour and a half maybe and, probably more"

"Eleven," he said angrily. "There's no way there's eleven in front of me."

"According to my list, you're twelfth," and I waved my piece of paper at him.

Hilda had been in the surgery earlier to collect some dressings before making her calls and, being the obliging woman she was, had noted down the names of the patients coming in and got out their charts to make things a bit easier for me.

Billy knew there was no point in arguing about that so he changed tack.

"My case is urgent. I'm in a bad way. I've a very bad complaint and could end up collapsing if I have to wait,"

He was crafty. He knew I couldn't expect him to divulge what his complaint was in front of the other patients. That would have been a breach of confidentiality. Billy had been around enough social services offices, benefits organisations and law courts to know what his rights were. He was way ahead of his time in that respect.

"In that case, if you feel your case is urgent, Mr Harper, you should let Nurse Armstrong know what it is and if she feels it is urgent, I will see you as soon as possible."

"I'm not telling no nurse nothing out here in this waiting room," Billy snapped. "The people will hear me. I have my rights to privacy the same as everybody else."

"You could whisper it to her," I said, more to annoy him than anything else.

"I'm whispering nothing to nobody. Who do you think I am whispering things to a nurse?" he said crossly.

"Well write it down on a piece of paper and show it to her."

"I can't write."

I found that hard to believe. A few days earlier I had seen him walking into his bookies reading the back page of a newspaper. To my mind, if a person can read a newspaper, they can almost certainly write unless they have some form of physically disability. I didn't want to get into an argument with him about whether he could read or not. He would lie through his teeth. He had a reputation as a liar. He was one of those individuals who believed in grabbing everything he could with both hands from the State and society and giving nothing back in return except cheek, rudeness and annoyance which he regarded as his right and entitlement.

"In that case, Mr Harper, if you cannot accept my suggestions, I cannot assess how urgent your case is. If Mrs Armstrong notices any deterioration in your condition, I'm sure she'll inform me," I said as I turned and went in to see Eugene.

Hilda told me later that if the other patients hadn't been so scared of Billy, they would have cheered at seeing the man put in his place.

When his turn came, he wasn't in any hurry and, like a grumpy bear, took his time. If he'd had to wait, well, so could anyone else who was coming after him. He lumbered up from his chair, and surveyed the other patients. He scratched his stomach slowly, then opened his mouth wide and let out an enormous belch. That seemed to give him a lot of satisfaction. He looked round at the other patients with a self-satisfied grin on his face and shambled into my office. As he slumped on to a chair, I thought, "for someone's who's supposed to be in a bad way and in a hurry, Billy Boy, you look as if you have all the time in the world."

"At long, long, long last," he grunted. "You're a lot slower than Roberts and he's slower than slow. You doctors have it easy, coming in here and sitting about and chatting to a few people for your big pay packets. I can tell you it's a nice wee earner and easy money if you can get it. Look how long I've been waiting while you've been in here enjoying yourself talking to people and raking in the money."

"Yes, Mr Harper," I replied. I am lucky getting all that money for doing next to nothing. It makes me almost feel ashamed of myself, earning so much for doing so little."

Billy was trying to irritate me with the easy job, nice little earner routine. I had found out the best way to deal with people like that is to agree with everything they say. There would have been no point in explaining to Billy I had been out for two hours at three o'clock that morning to a man dying from cancer or that the last patient to see me had been suicidally depressed and had needed a lot of time and effort to get him to agree to being admitted to a Psychiatric Hospital. Nor was there any point in telling him that, as soon as I finished my morning surgery, I had five home visits to make followed by a busy evening surgery as well as returning to see the grief stricken widow of the cancer patient while he sat about in Muldroon's lounge bar sinking his twelfth pint. There wouldn't be any visit to the sea that morning. Billy wouldn't have been interested in anything that didn't involve him. He didn't want to see anything beyond his own fat nose.

"So Mr Harper, what can I do for you?" I asked as Billy blew his nose noisily.

He wasn't in a hurry to tell me. He sniffed into his filthy handkerchief with exaggerated slowness. Billy had opted to wear a dirty string vest that morning instead of a shirt for his appointment with me. Now, as he laboriously cleaned his nose, I noticed a strong smell of body odour. Billy was a big fat man who sweated a lot and washed little. I didn't know how his wife put up with the smell of him but, then, she wasn't exactly odour free herself.

Nobody could ever accuse Billy of having any dress sense. He had on a baggy pair of green trousers that looked as though they'd been made from a tent. The trousers were tethered below his beer belly with a cord of binder twine. His dirty pair of wellington boots were covered in fresh cow manure. They had a good inch and a half of cow dung on them. A green trail had followed him into the consulting room. Fortunately the floors were covered in linoleum otherwise the stains would have been permanent. I don't think that would have bothered Billy too much even if he had noticed the trail. I wondered if he took off his boots before going into his own home.

Billy had tattoos all over his torso and all down his arms. He had done the tattooing on his fingers himself where he had etched out the words 'love' and 'hate' in thick blue lettering.

This was the first time I had dealt with Billy close up and I wasn't impressed. He came across as an ignorant, selfish boor of a man who had no respect for anything or anyone including himself. He had obviously set himself extremely low standards in life and hadn't come anywhere near attaining them.

When Dr O'Flathertie had commented on Billy's lack of manners he had added, "If you have any dealings with that pig of a man Harper, you will find that rudimentary social graces are absent."

That was obvious. I was irritated by him appearing in my office in a string vest. Maybe he had genuinely forgotten to put on a shirt but I doubted it. I wondered how any self respecting person could go to visit a professional person on a personal matter or visit anybody else for that matter about anything and only wear a string vest, Johnny Nelligan the town drunk had more self respect and dignity than that even when he was at his worst with the drink.

"Right mate," he said, "I'm not here to talk about you and your money. As far as I'm concerned you're under worked and overpaid and that's that. What I want is my cert."

"I'm sorry, Mr Harper, I didn't catch what you said."

Hilda had warned me he would be looking for a sickness certificate to remain off work for the rest of his life if he could get someone to give it to him.

"I said I want my cert. Is there something wrong with your hearing, mate?" he snapped.

I gritted my teeth. Billy would have tested the patience of Saint Patrick.

"The insolence of him," I thought, "coming in here, demanding a certificate to stay off work in that rude manner and his boots covered in cow muck from a morning's work."

I'd heard other patients saying that Billy had two jobs and didn't pay tax on either of them. They said he pretended he had a bad back and claimed he hadn't worked for five years. I wondered how he had managed to fool Dr Roberts for so long.

"What do you need a certificate for, Mr Harper?" I asked. I wasn't going to make it easy for him.

"What do you think I want a certificate for? To clean my china cabinet with?" he asked sarcastically.

"I'm not entirely sure. That's why I'm asking you."

"I need my certificate for the sickness benefit. That's what I need my certificate for."

He leaned forward and thumped his two fists down on my desk and glared at me. I never liked bullies and I wasn't about to start liking them now.

"Are you going to give me my certificate or not," he shouted. He looked and sounded menacing and he was a very big man. Maybe it wouldn't be such a good idea to tell him I didn't like his attitude.

"I will give you a certificate if you are entitled to one," I said firmly.

"I am entitled to one. Why do you think I've sat in that waiting room for two hours this morning, wasting my time while you dawdled through all those patients? Do you think I did it for fun or because I like sitting in waiting rooms?" he was roaring now.

"I will give you a certificate if you are entitled to one and, by that, I mean if you have a disease or injury or illness that prevents you from working."

"I have an injury. Can't you see I've a bad back? I'm entitled to a certificate and I want it now. It's all down on my chart about a bad back, why don't you read it. Dr Roberts has seen me hundreds of times with my back."

I looked at Billy's meagre notes. There was hardly anything written in them. Dr Roberts was like a lot of the old doctors of that time. He kept almost no notes. They all knew their patients intimately from living and working in the community and kept all the knowledge about them in their heads. It often made a locum's work really difficult as in right at that moment.

"You say Dr Roberts has seen you quite frequently about your back?"

"I said he's seen me hundreds of times. I was that bad with my back I had to go to Dublin with it and then stay in bed for six months at home?"

"How long ago was it that you injured your back?" I asked as I looked for a letter from the hospital. I couldn't find one. Maybe Dr Roberts kept that in his head too.

"How do I know how long? Look it up in the records," he snapped. He was getting more impatient and exasperated by the minute. At the same time I couldn't give a sickness note to someone simply because they demanded it and became menacing. Billy's records were almost blank except for a few recent notes made mostly by locums.

I found a brief note which had been made thirty seven years earlier on the day of his birth which said, 'Boy 13 pounds, Mother Para 8 severe PPH transferred Tralee.' In layman's terms that meant his mother delivered her ninth child, Billy, who weighed thirteen pounds at birth. Following the delivery, she lost a lot of blood – post partum haemorrhage (PPH) and had to be transferred to hospital because of that.

In the 1930s, the outlook for a mother with post partum haemorrhage was poor. There were no blood transfusions then and many women died shortly after birth from blood loss or a few days later from infection. I wondered what had happened to Billy's mother. Had she died shortly after his birth?

"Are you going to give me the cert or not?" Billy demanded, waking me from my reverie.

"I'll need to examine you first, Mr Harper if you don't mind."

"I do mind," he roared. "I mind a lot. It's all down on my file that I have a bad back and I need my certificate. I don't need no examinations."

"The reason I have to examine you is to see if there's been any improvement since you were last here," I explained.

"There's been no improvement, " he retorted. "It never gets any better for more than a day and then it's as bad as ever again. Sometimes I can walk about for a couple of days and everybody thinks there's nothing wrong with me and then bang, I'm as bad as ever, totally crippled for a week and I can't even get out of bed. Dr Roberts knows all about it. That's why he gives me certs."

I hadn't seen any evidence in the notes that Dr Roberts had ever issued Billy with a cert but I decided it wasn't the right time to mention that. There was a note from a locum several months previously for a six month certificate and a line written by Dr Roberts just before he went on holiday that read 'O/E NAD O cert nec' which meant, 'On examination nothing abnormal detected. No certificate necessary'

It seemed a strange thing for Dr Roberts to write if he was, as Billy claimed, issuing certificates regularly.

"That may be so, Mr Harper," I said, "but many people who have bad backs improve with time. You may not be aware but it is a legal requirement for me to examine you if I am to issue you with a sickness certificate. I have to see if there is any change for the better since the last time you were given one."

"Didn't you hear what I just told you? There isn't any change for the better. I'm ten times worse than I ever was. I'm in constant agony," Billy was almost screaming at me. He was one angry man. "I'm telling you I need that certificate or they'll cut my benefits off."

He was shouting louder and louder. I could imagine the patients in the waiting room enjoying the commotion. In one way, Billy's anger was working against him. For one thing, he was antagonising me and, for another, angry people often forget that they are supposed to be in pain and make elementary mistakes like shaking a fist in the doctor's face or scratching their heads in frustration when they have just told the doctor they can't move their arm.

"I really do have to examine you, Mr Harper, if I am to give you a certificate. It's an official, Government requirement," I insisted, speaking as calmly as I could. I was beginning to feel quite threatened by Billy's fury.

"When you say your back is sore," I went on when Billy didn't answer, "which part of your back do you mean?"

"I mean all of it. All of my back is sore," Billy snapped. "There's not one bit of it that isn't sore."

"Every bit of your back is sore? That sounds a bit unusual. Did you hurt your back in the past?"

"Of course I hurt it," he shouted. "How do you think I injured it unless I hurt it?"

I didn't quite follow his logic but felt sure Billy wouldn't be interested in explaining it.

I was finding this interview increasingly stressful, I suddenly decided all this annoyance over Billy's cert wasn't worth it. I'd either end up by getting a migraine or one of Billy's big fists in my face. Either way, I was going to be the loser.

"O.K. Mr Harper." I said abruptly. "I'm going to write you out a certificate."

"About time too, after all that carry on you've put me through," he said angrily. "You're far worse than the Big Doctor."

"The Big Doctor," I thought to myself, "that's the name the patients call the medical referee, the doctor who does spot checks on patients on long term sickness certificates.

All patients, whether they were malingerers or genuinely ill dreaded going to the Big Doctor in case he put them off the sick. The Big Doctor could overide a G.P.'s decision to issue a certificate if he thought the patient wasn't genuine. The Big Doctor in the Slievegart locality was particularly disliked. His name was Dr Vicard but everyone called him Dr Vicious. Dr Vicard didn't believe in sickness or sickness benefits and he put virtually every patient he saw off benefits both the bona fide and the chancers.

It suddenly came to me. The Big Doctor was the answer. I would ask Dr Vicard to call Billy in for an examination. He could do the dirty work. He'd put Billy off the sick and enjoy doing it into the bargain.

I was so pleased with myself at the idea that I nearly slapped Billy on the back.

"How long do you need?" I was feeling magnanimous now.

Billy looked at me in surprise. "A year," he said hesitatingly.

"What about two years Billy, wouldn't that be better, make your life a bit easier?"

Billy couldn't believe his luck.

"Yeh, two years would be O.K."

"Where's the thank you very much, Billy boy? You're not too quick with the gratitude are you?" I felt like saying as I quickly wrote out a certificate. Two years was better from my point of view too. As soon as Dr Vicard saw that he would be apoplectic and put Billy off the sick whether he deserved it or not. I signed the certificate with a flourish and handed it to Billy who grabbed it without a word. He got up and went out slamming the door behind him.

"And thanks to you too," I muttered as I heard him start up his car with a huge revving of the engine followed by a screech of tyres before he catapulted down the driveway.

As soon as the surgery was over, I got myself a cup of coffee and phoned Dr Vicard's office.

"Good morning," an unfriendly voice answered after one ring. "Dr Vicard speaking. Can I help you?" One thing about Dr Vicard, he didn't waste time on small talk.

"Hello Dr Vicard," I said, I almost said Dr Vicious. That would have got the conversation off to a very shaky start. "I'm sorry to disturb you. My name is Dr Griffin. I'm doing a summer locum for Dr Roberts in Slievegart."

"Are you now?" the lugubrious voice replied.

"Yes I am and the reason I'm phoning you is that I've just had one of Doctor Roberts' patients in to see me at my morning surgery."

"Did you now?" Dr Vicard asked with that doleful voice of his. The way he spoke you would have thought his whole family had just died.

"Yes I did and this man more or less demanded I gave him a sickness certificate."

"Did he now?" Dr Vicard's voice had gone up a tone from being morose to being morose and cross.

"Yes, Dr Vicard, he did. In fact he was a bit intimidating and threatening."

"Was he now?" Dr Vicard's voice had gone down an octave and sounded funereal as well as cross. I hoped he was cross with Billy and not with me. "And what was this Gentleman's name?"

"Billy Harper."

"Billy Harpoon?"

"No, Billy Harper."

"Billy Harper. You'd want to be thinking about speaking more clearly and not mumbling Dr Griffin. What's wrong with this Mr Harpoon?"

"A bad back, he says." I said as I thought "You'd want to be thinking about improving your communication skills and telephone manner, Dr Vicious."

"A bad back, you say. There's far too many bad backs around for my liking. The whole county seems to be going down with bad backs. They're everywhere you look. There seems to be an epidemic of bad backs." Dr Vicard spoke in a tone of voice that brooked no argument.

"And what did you find wrong with Mr Harpoon when you examined him, Dr Griffin?"

"Nothing, Dr Vicard.

"Nothing," he repeated.

"Nothing, although I have to say I didn't examine him."

"Didn't examine him," he said in astonishment.

"No, I didn't examine him......"

"You didn't examine him," Dr Vicard sounded appalled.

"No I didn't examine him but can I explain why, Dr Vicard," I said hastily. "I didn't examine him because I couldn't."

"You couldn't examine him, Dr Griffin."

"I couldn't examine him because he refused to let me."

"Refused to let you examine him?" Dr Vicard repeated in disbelief.

"Yes, refused."

"Refused, did he?" I could tell by the tone of his voice that he was very unhappy about that decision of Billy's.

"Yes, Dr Vicard, he absolutely and utterly refused to let me examine him. He had been going on about his human rights and when it came to examining him, he absolutely refused."

"His human rights and him on benefits," Dr Vicard thundered.

"That's Billy for you, Dr Vicard, he's very up to date with his rights."

"Is he now, Dr Griffin?"

"He is indeed, Dr Vicard." Dr Vicard's habit of repeating everything I said was beginning to unnerve me.

"I'm not a man for rights myself, Dr Griffin. There's too many rights about these days for my liking and I don't like people who like rights and I don't think I'm going to like Mr Harpoon."

"Do you think so?" I said pleased to be asking the question for a change.

"I do think so, indeed I do. Too many rights for too many people by far. Too many...."

"And another thing Dr Vicard, I think you ought to know about this man." I felt I had to interrupt him or he'd never have stopped talking about rights. He seemed to have a bee in his bonnet about them. "Even though he's been on benefits for the last few years, he has managed to hold down two jobs at the same time as well as claiming his benefits. When he came here this morning, he had fresh cow manure on his boots. I thought I ought to mention that to you not that I want to influence your decision or anything."

There was a lot of spluttering at the other end of the line. Dr Vicard didn't say anything for several seconds. I began to worry that something had happened to him, a small stoke or seizure perhaps. When he did speak, his voice was low and barely audible. It was like the soft gentle voice you hear in a horror movie and you know that the owner of the voice is neither soft nor gentle and that he or she is going to do something really wicked. I began to feel sorry for Billy.

"Fresh cow manure on his boots, you say," Dr Vicard said.

I never thought the words cow manure could be spoken with such venom.

"Yes, I'm afraid so, Dr Vicard."

"And did you issue Mr Harpoon, with the cow manure boots, a certificate, Dr Griffin?" His voice had gone back to being just plain nasty.

"I had to Dr Vicard. I was concerned for my safety. He's a big man. I felt he was a bit threatening."

"A big, threatening man, you say. Well let me tell you, Dr Griffin, big, threatening men don't scare me. I scare big, threatening men."

When Dr Vicard spoke like that, I couldn't help wondering if he maybe had some mental health issues himself. There was a finality to his words and I knew then, without a doubt, that Billy had no more chance of staying on his benefits than he had of becoming a snowman in hell.

160

"We'll have Mr Harpoon in here very soon, Dr Griffin, very soon indeed. Cow manure on his boots. We'll see about that, me and Mr Harpoon."

A few days later when I was doing the evening surgery, I heard the waiting room door crash open. I went out to see what was going on. Billy was standing in the middle of the room shaking like a jelly. There was no aggression in him now. He was almost too upset to speak. I called him straight into the surgery even though it wasn't his turn. He was so distressed I wondered if a member of his family had died.

"What's wrong, Billy?" I asked. "Has something happened to your family?"

"No, no, worse than that, far worse than that," he said. "That Doctor Vicious at the Medical Board has put me off the sick. Can you believe it and me with my bad back and almost a cripple."

"It's hard to take in," I said nodding my head sympathetically. To my surprise, I felt guilty. If anybody deserved to be off the sick it was Billy. Maybe I felt bad because he was taking it so badly.

"How did it all happen?" I asked.

"I got a call from that Doctor Vicious shortly after I left the surgery last week. He sounded very angry and wanted me to go in and see him that very same day to be examined. I hadn't even had the time to fill in the back of my cert, let alone send it to him. How did he know I was even given another cert?"

"From your last certificate, I suspect. He must have been working from that."

I wanted to distance myself from any thoughts Billy might have about my involvement in getting Dr Vicard to send for him.

"I told him I was far too sick to come in and see him. My back was in an awful state after leaving here and after all the fuss and nonsense you put me through. I told him I couldn't even get into my car, never mind drive. He said if that was the case, he would call round that evening. He was like a bloodhound the way he kept coming after me. I had to tell him about ten times it wouldn't be a suitable time before he would listen. I explained that my wife wasn't at all well and his calling round would upset and unsettle her and make her a lot worse. He agreed in the end but only after a lot of begging and persuading from me. He's one awkward, ignorant man.

"He gave me a time and a date to go and see him and told me not to be a minute late or he'd put me off the sick straight away without even examining me. I believed him, he sounded that nasty. He was waiting for me the minute I got out of my car. He met me at the front door of the Benefits Office when I went to see him today. He was angry before I even got to him. I'd heard from others who'd been to see him that he was a big man but he was more than big, he was massive. He was the biggest man I've ever seen in my entire life and ugly with it too. Every rugby player in Munster must have stood on that ugly face of his. He was contrary looking with it too, the contrarious man I ever met.

He rushed me up to his office without even saying hello, how are you, not a word. He asked me two questions and looked at my back for less than three seconds. One of the questions was, did I like milking cows. What sort of question is that for a doctor to ask? Does that Dr Vicious think he's working for the Milk Board? As soon as he'd finished looking at my back and that was all it was, a look, he told me there was nothing wrong with me and he was signing me off the sick permanently from that moment onwards.

"I tried to ask a question and he told me to shut up and said that his decision was final. How can he do that and me a sick man. I'm not fit to work and I've a family to rear. I need the Benefit's money or I'll never survive"

"It's a mystery to me, Billy that the Big Doctor's done that to you, a complete mystery and after me giving you a certificate only last week for two years. Those Big Doctors are a law unto themselves and we G.P.s can't go against them. Leave it to me and I'll see if there's anything I can do to help you," I said as I shook his hand and led him to the door. For some reason I couldn't explain, I felt guilty about Billy's predicament. Yet I had to think of all the people who genuinely needed the financial help and I knew Billy wasn't one of them. He had been defrauding the Benefits office for years probably for thousands of pounds, all paid for by the taxpayers. Some of that money could have come from the taxes I paid.

Over the next few days I began to feel quite pleased with myself for getting Billy off sick benefit and stopping him stealing all that money from the government but I did wonder once or twice why he had taken it so badly. I felt I had been a righteous citizen carrying out my medical duties correctly that was until I met Maggie.

Maggie was the social worker. She didn't call at the practice very often but, when she did, I enjoyed talking to her about her patients. She was efficient, sympathetic and had a good sense of humour. She came in for coffee one morning a few days after Billy had been put off the sick. She looked and sounded a bit cool towards me.

"I hear Billy Harper is off the sick, James," she said in a quiet voice. She was not her usual self. She wasn't laughing and joking like she generally did.

"Oh yes, he's off the sick alright. There's no doubt about that Maggie," I said as jovially as I could.

I wondered what was up with her and why she seemed so annoyed with me.

"I was a bit surprised to hear he was off the sick after Dr Roberts putting him on it for the last five years," she continued.

"Oh no, he didn't," I said. "The last time he came to the surgery, Billy got his certificate from a locum, not from Dr Roberts."

"I know that and that was a mistake," Maggie replied. "I'll explain to you. Four years ago, Dr Roberts gave Billy a sickness certificate to last him indefinitely. Billy only came to the locum to get it renewed when he was wrongly told by the Benefits office his certificate had been lost. It hadn't been lost at all and it turned out to be a bureaucratic mix up by the social services. Obviously the locum didn't want to give an indefinite certificate when she didn't know him and his full medical history so she gave him a certificate for six months."

I wondered how Maggie knew so much about Billy.

"Then why did Dr Roberts write O/E NAD O cert nec a few months after that?" I asked thinking I had caught her out.

"I know about that as well," Maggie said. "Dr Roberts wrote that note because Billy came to see him about another problem and Dr Roberts couldn't find anything particularly wrong with him regarding that so he wrote NAD concerning that problem. At the time, Billy asked Dr Roberts if he was sure he didn't need a new certificate. Dr Roberts told him that he didn't and that the old one would cover him indefinitely. That's why he wrote no cert necessary."

"How come you know so much about Billy and what he gets up to, Maggie?"

"I'll tell you how I know so much about him. Apart from being his family's social worker, I live about a mile from him and bump into him as well, maybe once or twice a week. We usually have a chat and he tells me everything that has happened to him since he last saw me. It seems to help him, being able to get his problems off his chest."

"Well then, seeing as you know him so well, do you think he should be on the sick with him holding down two jobs?" I asked. I could hardly keep the triumph out of my voice.

"How do you know he has two jobs, James?"

"Everybody knows it. It's the word on the street."

"The word on the street, James? I wouldn't have thought you would have paid much attention to that sort of gossip."

I began to feel embarrassed and could feel my face beginning to go red.

"Anyway, apart from that," I blundered on, "he had fresh cow dung all over his feet when he was here the other day, from milking the O'Neilly herd I presume and he was pretending his back was sore too."

"Are you sure he was at O'Neilly's farm?" Maggie asked. "I know for a fact he hasn't been there for two years. He has a cow of his own that he milks every morning. He uses the milk for his family and gives any extra to a neighbour. He probably got his wellingtons dirty from doing that. As for pretending his back is bad, well I know Billy can a bit of a chancer but he does get bad back pain if he does even the lightest of work, especially if he's annoyed or tired."

"Well, what about him helping Charlie O'Brien out in his market garden, " I persisted.

"Charlie O'Brien is his cousin. Billy gives Charlie a hand occasionally as much to get a break from the problems at home as anything else. Charlie gives him a sack of potatoes and a few vegetables for his trouble and little else every now and then."

I was beginning to feel bad about Billy. Had I made a blunder?

"Well, Maggie, do you think Billy should be on the sick?"

Maggie looked at me with her steady blue eyes. I could see she was about to say something but changed it into a cough. She cleared her throat and asked quietly, "Do you know anything about Billy's family life, James?"

"I know he's married and has two or three children and that he smokes and drinks at Muldoon's pub at lunch time once or twice a week."

I was choosing my words carefully now.

"Well that's true up to a point. He is married but he has six children, not two or three. One of his children, Brian is mentally and physically handicapped. He can do nothing for himself and often screams for hours on end in a high-pitched wail and that usually happens at night. Nobody knows why he does it and none of the pediatricians can find any medicine to calm him down.

When Brian starts screaming, Billy gets up and sits with him all night long. He nurses him and rocks him backwards and forwards. He seems to be the only one who can calm Brian down.

Billy's own childhood wasn't great either. His mother died soon after his birth. His father was a terrible alcoholic and abandoned his nine children when Billy was a year old. He never saw him again. He was in an orphanage for most of his childhood or living rough which explains his coarseness. Nobody ever taught him manners. Despite all that, he started a successful business in his late teens in Ballydehob but moved to Slievegart when he got married.

His wife, Marian, had a severe mental breakdown five years ago after the birth of their sixth child. She was in a psychiatric hospital for several months. She now gets bouts of mania which are difficult to control. The only way Billy can control her mania is to increase her medication until she is nearly in a stupor. It stops her running round like a mad thing but it means she is hardly capable of doing anything round the house. Billy does everything for her and the children and he is often in agony with his back."

As Maggie continued, I felt worse by the minute, I thought of the problems I had created for Billy by getting his benefits cut off. How could I have been so horrible to think his wife was smelly when she was incapable of washing herself.

"Have you been down to their house, James?"

I nodded my head dejectedly. She was going to tell me they lived in a tumble down tree house full of angry gorillas and had no electricity or running water. I was nearly right.

"I'll tell you how they live. They live in an old wet, two bed-roomed house near a swampy bog that is infested with rats and midges. Up to four years ago they had no running water and had to draw their water from a muddy stream that runs through the bog. The house was condemned but the farmer that owns it is a decent, generous man. He lets them live in it rent free as long as they don't ask him to fix it up because he can't afford to.

Without that house they would be homeless while they wait for a council house to become available locally. You know there aren't any available in this area, nor are there likely to be for a long time. It would be detrimental to Marion's health if they moved out of this area. Any changes in her life seem to upset her mental equilibrium.

"Right, right, that's enough" I felt like shouting. I didn't want to hear any more about what a bad man I'd been getting Billy's benefits cut off when he had enough on his plate already. But there was no stopping Maggie now that she had started. Her initial coolness towards me had thawed. She was talking animatedly now.

"To make matters worse, Marion's parents decided to come and look after her, uninvited I might add. They left their house in Ballymaher and moved their caravan next to Bill's home. The father is a fairly reasonable man when he's not drinking which isn't too often but the mother-in-law is an interfering, impossible woman who's always poking her nose into everything and never gives Billy a moment's peace. He has had to carry his father-in-law to the caravan when he has collapsed with the drink and I can't count the number of times that has happened. That wrecks his back for days but he still does it the next time. No wonder he goes for a drink himself when he's got the money. Wouldn't you?"

"O.K., O.K. Maggie," I said, "I get the message. I've made a mistake, a bad mistake."

"Do you think so?" Maggie said with a touch of sympathy. "But there's more. Did you know that Billy was one of the hardest workers in this entire county even after hurting his back but it was the birth of Brian followed by his wife's mental illness that broke him. If it hadn't been for those setbacks, he would have made something of himself. You should have seen him fifteen years ago. He was a fine figure of a man before he let himself go. Then he became overweight and morose and just didn't care any more. Every day for him is just another day trying to survive. I know he comes across as a total ignoramus but his heart is good, one of the best although, to be honest, it took me a long time to find it. The bottom line James, is, how many people do you know who would put up with what he has had to put up with or would do what Billy does for his wife and son and his in laws, week in and week out and never a word of complaint?"

I felt embarrassed I had put Billy through so much but to be fair, I wouldn't have done what I did if I had known his circumstances.

"Five years ago, Dr Roberts thought Billy was on the verge of a serious nervous breakdown trying to hold down a job with his bad back and keep the family together. He went down to Billy's house and told him he was putting him on the sick indefinitely whether he liked it or not. Billy wasn't on for it at all but Dr Roberts explained the financial implications. It turned out Billy was better off on his benefits and allowances than if he worked."

"Right, Right Maggie," I said raising my voice above hers, "stop right there. That's enough. You're making me feel like I'm the baddest man in Ireland. Basically what you are trying to tell me is I've goofed up and Billy should be signed back on the sick as soon as possible."

"Yes, that would be nice, "Maggy said with a smile.

"Are you going anywhere near Billy's house soon or will I leave the certificate down there myself."

"As it happens, I'm going down there this evening," Maggie said.

"O.K. then, can you give him this?" and I hastily scribbled out a certificate.

Thank you," she said as she put it in her pocket. "Can you just tell me one thing, James. How are you going to sort this all out with Dr Vicious."

"Dr Vicious?" I asked.

"Yes, the Big Doctor that Billy mentioned to me. He seems quite a difficult man. By the sound of him, he has his own problems."

"Oh, that Dr Vicious. Don't you worry about him. I'll deal with him," I said as I thought if Dr Vicious and myself had taken a full history of Billy and not jumped to conclusions, we would have saved Billy a lot of trouble. At the same time though, if Billy had attempted to show even the most basic of manners, he wouldn't have got my back up and he could have saved himself an awful lot of trouble too.

I felt relieved as Maggie drove off. The problem had been resolved although I still had an unpleasant confrontation with Dr Vicard to look forward to. Still, I thought wearing a string vest without a shirt when you go to see a doctor isn't the best way to gain his sympathy especially if the doctor thinks you're trying to pull a fast one on him.

As my old Grandmother used to say - Civility costs nothing.

The Demon Drink

The door of the chapel flew open with a loud bang. I looked round to see what was going on and was astonished to see a donkey standing in the open doorway. The donkey looked nearly as startled as I did. There was a lot of noise and shouting coming from somewhere behind the donkey.

I was towards the back of the chapel and caught a glimpse of a cloth cap on the head of a rough looking man in dark clothes. He was pushing the donkey from behind, trying to get it into the chapel.

"Come on Ned, get yourself moving," the man was shouting. "Get yourself in there you dirty beast of an animal. We're going to be late for Mass if you don't get a move on. Hurry yourself up. You know as well as I do Father McKinley hates late comers so get yourself in there."

Ned was doing all he could to not get in there. He was resisting all attempts to push him from behind. A few people along from me sniggered. One man raised his eyes to heaven and said, "Would you believe it? 'Ole Johnny Nelligan's on the drink again. He must have hit it hard if he's trying to bring his donkey to Chapel in the middle of Mass."

Meanwhile, Johnny was getting more and more exasperated and Ned was getting more and more determined not to budge.

"Come on, you stupid animal, you're keeping me late for Mass and that'll be another black sin on my immortal soul and it'll be all because of you and your pig headedness."

I recognised the slurred voice then. Johnny Nelligan was the town drunk. He was drunk every day but every now and then he would go on terrible binges when he would stagger around blind drunk for days doing the most ridiculous things like he was doing right then.

Johnny suddenly produced a stick and started whacking the donkey across his back but there wasn't much strength in his arm and Ned didn't budge an inch.

"Come on, come on Ned and get moving like a good lad or I'll lay this stick down hard on your stubborn frame. We could be in time yet if you moved yourself," he shouted.

It only made Ned more stubborn, in fact he took a couple of steps backwards and Johnny sat down with a look of surprise on his face.

By this time, the Church was in pandemonium. Everyone was straining to see what was going on. Father McKinley had stopped in the middle of his sermon and was staring down the central aisle to see who was making the noise. He stared in disbelief at the sight of a drunk man trying to bring a donkey into his Sunday Mass. There was a buzz of excitement from the congregation. This was certainly more entertaining than Father McKinley's sermon.

Father McKinley got over his astonishment and found his voice. He had a very loud voice. It roared down the length of the Church.

"What do you think you're doing, Johnny Nelligan, bringing a dirty animal into God's own home on a Sunday morning in the middle of Holy Mass. It's a profanity, a blasphemy, a sacrilege, an obscenity a....a..a..." his voice petered out. He was lost for words.

Johnny looked up from his exertions. He'd heard the priest shout but hadn't heard what he had said.

"I'm sorry, Father, for the delay and holding up the Mass. I'll have Ned inside in a jiffy if you just hold on a minute with the sermon like."

"Get that brute out of here NOW," Father McKinley yelled.

Johnny still didn't hear him. He was too intent in hauling himself back to his feet and shoving the donkey forward.

"I'm sorry, Father, if you're in the middle of your sermon and I've interrupted you but I've one obstinate donkey here who won't come in to Mass. He must have Protestant blood in him. Maybe you could see your way to baptising him after Mass."

Johnny rambled on and on in a drunken haze. He didn't realise how cross Father McKinley was becoming.

"We'll have him inside in a minute, Father. If you could only get some of the St Vincent de Paul men to help me, we'd be a lot quicker."

He went back to shooing the donkey forward but the donkey had put his feet more firmly on the ground than ever and had started to bray loudly.

That did it for the congregation. The quiet giggles that the worshippers had been trying to hold in out of respect for the chapel and for fear of Father McKinley's temper erupted into laughter. A braying donkey with Protestant blood in him coming to Mass was too much for them and, once they had started laughing, they couldn't stop, everybody, that is, except Father McKinley. His face was like thunder. He was storming down the middle of the aisle, his face crimson with rage beneath his flaming red hair. One look at him was enough to wipe the smiles off a lot of faces.

Johnny was so drunk he still didn't notice. His vision was affected by drink as much as the rest of him.

"Are you coming to help me, Father?" he called out as he saw the priest approaching. "Now aren't you the gentleman no matter what the people say about you and your fondness for drink yourself and you being as cross as a bag of weasels. But no matter, we all have our little faults. People say I drink too much too, you know......" Johnny was getting into his stride.

"Father," he babbled on, "we'll maybe leave the baptism until after Mass if that's alright with you, not to hold things back too much for all these lovely people," and he squinted at the congregation.

Father McKinley reached the donkey and slapped it across the jaw. It turned and bolted knocking Johnny to the ground. He clambered to his feet and stood there swaying on his feet. Father McKinley was a very big man. I could well believe the rumours that he was a descendant of Brian Boru, the High King of Ireland. He towered over little Johnny. He was so cross that when he spoke, spit flew out of his mouth.

"Get that filthy creature out of my Church and out of my grounds you... you... you stupid, drunk, old man. Get yourself out, right now, and that animal of yours.... the both of you."

Johnny looked up in surprise. It wasn't the greeting he had been expecting.

"Ah now, Father McKinley," he said, "that's no way to be talking about Ned and him so sensitive. Can he not come in for a minute and get your blessing. I can see by your attitude, baptism is out of the question and we'll leave it so, but a blessing......."

Father McKinley's blue eyes flashed with anger. His mouth was fixed in a scary grimace.

"There'll be no baptism and no blessings of any kind and I'm giving you thirty seconds to have that animal out of my chapel and off the Church property or I'll call the Gardai and have them arrest you for disturbing the peace."

Father McKinley was like a lot of red headed people, irascible when he got upset and there was no doubting that Father McKinley was very upset. It was true he liked his drop of whiskey in the evening but his drinking was nowhere near Johnny's level. He was a tolerant man and showed tolerance to many things but there was one area where he drew the line and that was if anyone showed disrespect to God or his Church. That made him livid but Johnny, in his drunken state wasn't aware of how angry Father McKinley was.

"Will you not let us come in at least for a little bit of a prayer, Father, and then we'll be on our way," he pleaded.

"There'll be no donkey praying in my Church," Father McKinley roared. "Get out, get out ...... NOW." His face had turned purple.

I knew from his visits to the surgery that Father McKinley had very high blood pressure, probably brought on by getting so uptight over little things and by drinking whiskey each evening to calm down his over strung nerves and get a night's sleep. Johnny's shenanigans were just the sort of situation that could send his blood pressure through the roof. His father had died at a similar age with a stroke brought on by stress. I didn't want the same thing to happen to Father McKinley. I got up from my seat and went across to him and gripped him by the elbow.

"Look, Father," I said, "a few of the men here will get Johnny and the donkey out of the chapel if you'll just go back to the Parochial House and settle yourself down for a few minutes. Johnny and his donkey will be gone and away before you know it."

Father McKinley stared at me unseeingly for several seconds. I could see the whole episode had deeply upset him. Despite his irascibility and failings, he was a good man who had a deep love for his parishioners and God and the Church. He was known throughout Kerry for that profound belief and love. Anyone who insulted God, insulted Father McKinley on a very personal level. He was loyal to his friends and God was his best friend. In Father McKinley's eyes, Johnny had slapped God's face and he was having none of it.

I shook his arm again trying to get some sort of response. He slowly came round like a man coming out of a faint.

"Look Father," I said, "you really do need to go back to the parochial house and get your house keeper to make you a cup of tea and rest yourself for a few minutes. The St Vincent de Paul men will get Johnny and Ned on their way as quickly as they can. I'll get my medical bag and check your blood pressure once that's sorted out."

I asked his housekeeper, who had been sitting in the front pew and had come to see if she could help, to go with him and get him settled down.

Once I had Father McKinley organised I went outside to find Johnny protesting vehemently about himself and Ned being forcibly removed from the Church grounds.

"Ned has every right in the world to go into that Chapel. He was born and bred in Slievegart which is more than can be said for a lot of you. He's never committed a sin in his entire life which is something none of you can lay claim to. I think you know what I'm talking about Swindler Sweeney," he said turning to look at a local business man.

Dominic Sweeney turned pale at Johnny's words. There was a sudden rush to force Johnny out before he spilt the beans on any one else. He was dragged to the chapel gates and Ned was driven along in front of him braying at every step he took.

"Don't you hear poor Ned lamenting?" Johnny shouted as he was bundled into the lane beside the chapel and encouraged to get himself away home. "Don't you hear my poor donkey keening and crying like a baby. That's because he's hurt by your unchristian, uncharitable and uncalled for treatment of himself and me."

A few of us escorted them to the end of the lane. He pleaded with us to ask Father McKinley to let Ned go to confession if he wouldn't let him go to Mass.

Years of drinking had pickled his brain and permanently damaged it. His conception of what was real and what wasn't was distorted along with his memory.

"Please ask Father McKinley one more time," he begged with tears in his eyes. "Let Ned make his first confession. It'll only take a minute and it doesn't have to be today. We can arrange a date for it. You see Ned has hardly a sin on his soul. He has the soul of an angel. It's as white and pure as the driven snow apart from his stubbornness that is, that being the nature of the animal but obstinacy is still a sin and I want Ned to confess to it before he meets his Maker."

I didn't think there would be much point in telling Johnny in his present drunken state that even if we surmounted the ecclesiastical difficulties of a donkey going to confession, there would still be the communication problems to deal with.

I grabbed my medical bag out of the Landrover as we went past. One of the men managed to persuade Johnny to get into his car after he promised to return straight away for Ned.

I went up to the parochial house and checked Father McKinley's blood pressure. As I suspected, it was dangerously high, I told him he needed to lie down for a few hours and finish his Mass another day. He was still agitated by Johnny's behaviour and wouldn't hear of it.

"The people of Slievegart are not going to be denied their Sunday Mass by a donkey and the asinine carry on of its owner," he stormed. "Mass will resume in five minutes."

It was only by getting Mary Agnes, his house keeper to talk to him in her forthright manner that made him listen to reason.

A few days later, I was going into a shop in the main street when I saw Johnny slumped in a doorway, an empty whiskey bottle lying beside him. Ned was nowhere to be seen. Johnny looked up as I went by. He wasn't as drunk as he usually was at that time of the day.

"You're one of the young lads that threw me out of the chapel the other day, aren't you?"

I was surprised he recognised me considering how drunk he had been at the time.

"Well let me tell you something, laddie. I'm sorely annoyed with myself for that carry on with Ned. What would my poor mother have said if she'd seen that? She'll be turning in her grave if not spinning in it at the very idea of one of her sons insulting the clergy and her memory by trying to bring a donkey to Mass"

I felt sorry for the old man. He sounded genuinely upset.

"As it is," he went on, "I'm full of shame for my drinking and it's a cross I've had to bear ever since my behaviour killed my own lovely mother. Do you see this?" and he held up the empty whiskey bottle. "Well that's the last drop of drink that is ever going to pass my lips, the last drop I will ever touch even if it kills me."

I'd heard that sort of promise many a time before, especially from someone like Johnny who had been known to drink three bottles of whiskey in a day so I didn't pay much heed.

"Well, that's good to hear, Johnny, I'm delighted you're coming off the drink," I said.

"You don't believe me, young lad, do you? I hardly believe it myself but it's the truth. Still, I don't blame you," Johnny said with a wry smile. "You're not the first I've said it to today and you'll not be the last but it's the truth before God. I'll never touch another drop of drink as long as I live. I'll tell you this and I'll tell you no more. If my lovely mother was alive today, she'd turn in her grave. I'm going off the drink in reparation for the annoyance I caused her in her lifetime."

Johnny must have told everyone he met in Slievegart he was giving up the drink. It was the talk of the town. In his fifty-year alcoholic career, nobody had ever heard him make such a claim before. It was a couple of days later when I had just sat down to a big salmon steak for my tea when Hilda came to the door.

"I'm sorry to trouble you, James," she said, "but I just called in to see Johnny Nellligan on my way home. I hadn't seen him about the town for a day or two and I was wondering if he had actually tried giving up the drink after all that talk of his. I found him in an awful state. He's huddled up in his bed with his back against the wall babbling away like a maniac. He seems scared out of his wits about something and nothing he says makes any sense. He must be going through a dose of the D.T.s. I think he ought to go to the hospital tonight or he'll never make it through to the morning.

Delirium tremens, or the D.T.s as it is more generally known is a reaction the human body undergoes when alcohol is suddenly withdrawn from someone who regularly drinks heavily. It is characterised by wild shaking (tremens) of the body especially the head and limbs. The patient is extremely restless and confused. They may not even recognise people they know and often get delusional ideas. These delusions are frequently terrifying especially when they are accompanied by hallucinations. In the past, before D.T. patients were hospitalised, many of them died from dehydration. They simply couldn't hold a cup or their head steady enough to take a drink because of the tremors. Without treatment the huge tremors can go on for days. They exhaust the patient and frail patients can sometimes die from heart failure.

"Right then," I said to Hilda, "I'll be with you in a moment."

I took the salmon steak back to the kitchen and put it in the fridge. I put on my jacket and we went to see Johnny.

He lived in an old, run down cottage at the edge of town. His electricity had been cut off long ago because he hadn't paid his bills. It was the dirtiest house I had ever been to. Empty beer and whiskey bottles littered every spare inch of space. I saw a grubby table with a loaf of stale bread and some rancid butter on it. That seemed to have been Johnny's staple diet apart from the calories he took in from his alcohol consumption.

Johnny was hunched up on his bed with his knees drawn up to his chin. He was shaking uncontrollably and jabbering incoherently as he stared in terror at the opposite wall. The sheets he was sitting on and had partly pulled up towards his face as if to protect him, were brown with dirt. They hadn't been washed in years. I shook his shoulder to attract his attention but he didn't look round.

"What's wrong, Johnny?" I asked. "Are you alright?"

"Look, look, can you not see them?" He shrieked in terror as he pointed at the wall. "There's hundreds of them and they're coming for me. They're crawling up and down the wall and they're coming for me. For the love of God stop them. If you've an ounce of sympathy in you, please, please, stop them."

"What's coming for you, Johnny?" I asked quietly trying to calm him down.

"They are. They are. Can't you see them. Rats and fleas and vermin, hundreds and thousands of them running down that wall and all over the floor and they're coming to get me," and Johnny started brushing at his clothes in absolute terror as if he was trying to shake off the rats and vermin or whatever he thought was crawling all over him.

He was so frightened I thought he would take a heart attack right in front of our eyes. I drew up a syringeful of diazepam and, with a great deal of difficulty, managed to give it to him intravenously. Hilda had to sit on his arm to get it to stay anywhere near steady enough to give the injection.

The diazepam settled him a little and Hilda rushed off to call an ambulance. When it arrived, Johnny wasn't able to stand, let alone walk as his legs were shaking so much. We eventually managed to get him outside. When the back door of the ambulance was opened, he screamed and screamed.

"Close the doors, close the doors. Quick. The cockroaches are coming for me along with the rats. They're crawling all over me. Help me. Please help me. Get them off me. Please somebody help me."

I had never seen anyone in the throes of alcohol withdrawal before. It was one of the most alarming and frightening conditions I had ever seen. Hilda was almost in tears. I was afraid Johnny would take a convulsion before the ambulance could get him to hospital. The ambulance crew almost dragged Johnny into the ambulance despite his screaming protests about cockroaches and rats pulling at his skin.

When I phoned the hospital the next day, I was told he'd had a restless night and had taken a major convulsion in the early hours of the morning. The doctors had found it hard to bring it under control.

I went to see Father McKinley about Johnny. He had recovered his composure by then and, being the charitable man he was, went at once to see him in Tralee Hospital. I asked him what he thought of Johnny when he came back.

"To tell you the truth, Dr Griffin," he said, "I don't think Johnny has long for this life. I was shocked and saddened by the appearance he was in, an awful state altogether. There was that look of death about him that I've seen before. He made his peace with God in his own way and asked me to make sure Ned is well looked after and brought up a good Catholic." Father McKinley paused for a moment and looked at me. I was wondering how he had taken that death bed wish of Johnny's when a smile came to his face. Maybe Father McKinley had a sense of humour after all.

"Now tell my one thing, Dr Griffin, and you being a University man might know the answer to this," he said as he stood up to leave.

"Yes Father?" I said flattered he should think so highly of me.

"How do you bring a donkey up to be a good Catholic?"

Poor old Johnny died two days later, He took several more convulsions and then developed pneumonia. It was all too much for an old man like him who had abused his body for so long. Johnny was far from perfect but when he died, a little spark of life and humour went out of Slievegart for ever.

"The demon drink, the Devil's buttermilk, life's elixir, the water of life, the hooch, fire water, whatever you like to call it, James, has claimed another victim," was how Dr O'Flahertie explained it to me as he knocked back his third gin and tonic in a row. "And it'll not be the last either by a long shot, in your life time or mine, who will die from the effects of too much liquor."

I had no answer to that.

The Nursing Home

Slievegart was one of the first towns in Ireland to have a nursing home. In the 1960s and 70s most people, when they could no longer manage on their own and look after themselves would be cared for by one of their daughters or a son and his wife. If they had no relatives, they went into a long stay hospital, generally an old Victorian building that had been a work house in earlier times.

The nursing home in Slievegart was called Avila. It was run by a prim and proper lady called Miss Eugenie Grieg. Miss Grieg had been a matron in a private hospital in Dublin for many years. She still dressed as one and insisted that all her female staff wear dark blue uniforms similar to the ones her nurses had worn in Dublin. Everything was done by the book. Beds had to be made in a certain way and that way only. Breakfast was at eight o'clock sharp, lunch at twelve and tea at five o'clock. Tea breaks were at three pm and nine pm. Lights were out at ten o'clock.

Miss Grieg was a big woman who rarely smiled. She wasn't unkind but she was a stickler for rules and she was firm, very firm. If any of the residents acted up, they were put in their place. They weren't quite given a verbal warning followed by a written one but they were made aware that whatever misdemeanour they had committed would not be tolerated unless they had a good reason for it. Misdemeanours included leaving your toothbrush or dentures in the bathroom, not flushing the toilet after using it or saying you didn't like your lunch. Miss Grieg prided herself on providing a clean, warm home with wholesome food for her charges. The atmosphere was calm, controlled and peaceful.

Most of the residents were very happy there. Among her family, Eugenie was called Blossom, although she was always called Miss Grieg in the nursing home. Her attitude was that if you didn't like Avila, then she could show you to the nearest bus stop. Most of the residents took to the home like ducks to water. For several of the old men who had never married, it was the first time that anyone had looked after them since they were children.

Dr Roberts had neglected to let me know before his hasty departure that he called at the nursing home once a week on a Monday afternoon to do a ward round and see any patient that required attention. I was phoned promptly at nine o'clock on my second Monday in Slievegart.

"Good morning, Doctor, Miss Grieg of Avila speaking. I hope you will be coming to see us this afternoon," she said in a manner that suggested I had no alternative.

I wondered who or what Avila was. The only Avila I had ever heard of was a town in Spain where the mystical Saint Teresa of Avila had lived.

"Good morning, Miss Grieg," I replied, "could you please just clarify who is expecting to see me?"

"Avila Nursing Home, of course." There was a hint of disapproval in her voice. "Surely you are aware of my Nursing Home. Did Doctor Roberts not inform you of your duties here before his departure?" she asked sharply.

"I think Dr Roberts was in a bit of a hurry when he was leaving, Miss Grieg otherwise, I am sure he would have mentioned Avila"

"In that case, I'd better explain. Each Monday afternoon at half past two sharp, Dr Roberts visits Avila and deals with any medical problems we might have encountered in the preceding week. Do you think you could ...."

"Yes, yes of course. I'll call today, Miss Grieg," I interrupted, relieved that was all I had to do. I quite liked the idea of going round and chatting to a few old folk. I liked hearing their life histories and having a bit of a laugh with them. Most of the elderly people that I'd had dealings with had a good sense of humour and didn't take themselves too seriously.

"Two thirty then, Doctor Griffin," Miss Grieg said primly.

"Two thirty it will be," I replied.

"Goodbye," she said and put the phone down. Blossom obviously wasn't a woman to waste time on small talk.

I pulled up outside Avila at twenty five minutes past two that afternoon. I didn't think Miss Grieg would be too pleased if I was late especially on my first visit. The Nursing Home was on the outskirts of the town on the coast road. It was surrounded by well-tended gardens. There was an immediate impression of space and light. All the walls were white washed. I liked its welcoming atmosphere. As I pushed open the glass door, I saw a notice which read, "Please ensure when you are leaving that you only leave with whoever you came with."

Did they really think someone was going to run off with some of the patients or perhaps even Blossom?

I made my way to Miss Grieg's office and knocked on the door.

"Enter." It was the same stern voice of the phone call.

I pushed open the door to find Matron in full dark blue uniform and white starched apron and hat sitting behind a mahogany desk examining medical files. Everything in the room was exactly as it should be, not a thing was out of place.

"Ah, Doctor Griffin, how kind of you to call at such short notice." She shook my hand and smiled briefly. It almost made her look pleasant. "Now let's begin. I have three patients I would like you to review this afternoon."

She put three folders on to a trolley which she then began to push out of the door and along the corridor. I had to half gallop to keep up with her. Blossom was not one to hang about.

"I would like you to examine Mrs O'Leary in Room one. She has quite advanced dementia but she seems to have become a lot more confused over the weekend. I think she might have a chest or urinary infection that has decompensated her.

I was impressed by Miss Grieg's efficiency and she seemed to know her medicine.

"Mrs O'Leary is a charming old lady with a very poor memory. She realises there is something wrong with her memory but she's not quite sure what. She's usually very good at pretending to be normal but not today. That's why I think she might have an infection."

I went into the room and found a charming, elegant old lady in a pink night dress lying on top of her bed reading a newspaper. She looked perfectly normal to me.

"Good morning," Mrs O'Leary said putting her paper down. "Are you the plumber I've been phoning all weekend to come and fix my lavatory?"

"Not exactly, Mrs O'Leary," I said shaking her hand, "I'm the doctor. I'm here to see if you might have a chest infection."

"Are you really? That's very nice of you to come and see me and you so busy too, such a nice young man." She kept holding my hand as she spoke.

"Now, Mrs O'Leary," I said trying to get her to let go of my hand. "I need to go round to the other side of your bed to examine you if that's alright with you."

"Oh, that's fine by me," she said still holding on to my hand.

I tried to gently ease my hand free but she gripped it tighter.

"No, no, I don't mind at all. It's ever so nice of you to call. She gave me a lovely smile and strengthened her hold on my hand.

"If you could just let my hand go, Mrs O'Leary, It might make things easier."

"What do you mean?" She declared crossly. "I'm not holding your hand you impertinent young man. How dare you say that? I'll have you know I am not in the habit of holding strange men's hands, particularly plumbers who have called to fix my lavatory." She flung my hand away from her as if she had suddenly noticed she was holding a cow pat in it.

As I walked round to the other side of the bed, I noticed Miss Grieg's shoulders shaking slightly.

Mrs O'Leary lay on her bed with a contented smile staring at Miss Grieg. She seemed to have forgotten me already. I touched her gently on the arm to let her know I was there. She seemed startled and gave a little shriek.

"Who are you and where have you come from?" she asked. "Have we met before? You must be the plumber about the faulty lavatory. Is that who you are?"

"Not exactly, Mrs O'Leary," I said as I looked at Matron who was doing her best not to laugh and getting redder in the face with the effort. Maybe she wasn't so bad after all.

I prescribed antibiotics and was pleased to find Mrs O'Leary's memory had improved a little when I called the following week.

After I had seen the other two patients, Miss Grieg took me into the dispensary to wash my hands. She handed me a crisp white towel to dry them and then escorted me back to her office where a tray with a china pot full of piping hot Earl Grey tea and a plate of warm scones bursting with cherries and smothered in butter was waiting for us.

After that I really enjoyed the Monday afternoon ward rounds. I usually saw between three and five patients. One of my favourites was an old doting lady called Sadie who wiped her feet before she went outside for her daily stroll with one of the nurses but refused to wipe them when she came back.

Sadie was inclined to wander and the nursing home doors had to be locked to keep her safe. Maybe that was the reason for the notice on the front door. She liked to drop in and visit the other residents at any time of the day or night which could be a bit disruptive. I had to give her some nighttime sedation so that everybody else could get some sleep.

Sadie's big interest in life was food. As soon as one meal was over, she looked forward to the next. Part of the reason for her being so friendly with the other residents and visiting them so often was that it gave her the opportunity to lift the grapes and biscuits from their bedside tables. She had put on three stone in weight since she had come in to Avila six months earlier and that's a lot when you're barely five foot tall. The staff had a tricky problem with Sadie trying to control her eating habits.

Every time Sadie saw me arrive, or any other visitor for that matter, she would waddle up in her carpet slippers and floral dress and plant herself directly in front of us. She would put her hands on her hips and look up before asking earnestly, "Have you had your dinner yet?"

I would invariably say I hadn't because it made her so happy to be able to tell me that she'd had hers and that she was going to have her tea soon. Once she had imparted that bit of news, she would shuffle off down the corridor in search of more food. The Nurses called these foraging raids "Sadie's snack attacks".

One Friday afternoon, I was called to Avila to see an elderly gentleman who was dying. He had been quite well in the morning but after lunch had become weak and breathless. By the time I arrived, he was unconscious and his breathing was shallow. Matron had sent for his relatives.

Mr William Forsythe was of Anglo Irish extraction. He had been a wealthy business man and a land owner in his heyday. I had heard some vague rumblings about a family dispute which had resulted in Mr Forsythe signing himself into Avila several years earlier.

Mr Forsythe died shortly after my arrival and Matron asked me to call into her office on my way out to sign his death certificate. I thought she seemed a little tense.

"Look Dr Griffin," she said. She always called me Dr Griffin, never James but then I would never have dreamt of calling her Blossom. "We have a bit of a problem regarding Mr Forsythe's death. It's important I explain it to you in the light of possible future events."

It all sounded mysterious and full of intrigue.

"Eight years ago, before he came here, Mr Forsythe signed various pieces of his property over to his four sons to avoid inheritance tax. As a result of that, there was a dispute between the sons and basically, none of them talk to each other but, oddly enough, they have all remained faithful to their father. They seem to blame each other for what they consider an unfair division of his property but none of them blame the old man though I have to say, they all seemed to have been dealt with generously and are very wealthy men. Over the years they have visited him regularly, though never at the same time unless by accident when the second brother to arrive will go for a drive until the first one has gone.

"Now you've seen what a lovely old gentleman Mr Forsythe was and it upset him terribly to see his sons fall out. He thought, and I'm inclined to agree with him, that he'd treated them all fairly. The sons thought differently and that explains why he left his manor house and came to live here. He wanted to have some peace and quiet in his old age and to distance himself from the squabbling which he couldn't get his sons to resolve, no matter what he did. My problem is that they will all be arriving in the next hour or two to see their father's remains and that is going to create problems. As I mentioned, none of the brothers speak to each other and we've found that very difficult to deal with on the odd occasion when they've all arrived here at the same time.

They're all big men in their forties and they behave like spoilt pre-school children.

"They are all stubborn men too and each will insist on taking their father's remains to their own homes for a traditional wake. Mr Forsythe was completely opposed to them arguing over where his body was going to go after his death and, sensible man that he was, he wrote into his will where his remains were to be taken. They're to be taken from Avila to a funeral parlour in Cork City. Anyone who wants to see his remains must go there. The funeral arrangements down to the last hymn have all been organised. His remains are to go straight from the funeral parlour to the Church and from the Church to the cemetry. Refreshments for the guests have been arranged in a hotel in the centre of Cork.

"My problem is that these men are, for want of a better word," and Matron's voice faltered a little, "a bunch of snotty, stuck up, male, chauvinist pigs."

I was taken aback by her choice of words. It wasn't what I expected to hear from someone who was so straightlaced.

"I'm sorry to use those words to describe Mr Forsythe's sons but that's the only way I can describe them. They believe nothing I say to them and, not to put too fine a point on it, that's simply because I'm a woman. It's difficult to understand how such Victorian attitudes can still exist in today's world when we've just been through the swinging sixties and a so called sexual revolution and militant feminism but they do exist, and very strongly in the Forsythe men."

"Why didn't the father tell them his wishes before he died?" I asked.

"Oh that would only have intensified the feud. These men all have massive egos and are unbelievably touchy."

"Then why can't you show them the will their father left and let them see his instructions."

"Unfortunately I can't. Believe me, nothing would give me greater pleasure than to see them being put in their place by a woman but the instructions regarding the burial are not here at present. I know the instructions off by heart as I discussed them with Mr Forsythe myself so often. He didn't expect to die so soon and he'd sent his will off to an old friend just two days ago for his opinion and that's why the papers are not to hand."

"Now where you come in, Dr Griffin and I hope you won't mind obliging me and I would be most grateful if you did. Would you please meet these men and tell them exactly what their father wanted and make them see some sort of reason. They are the sort of men that will only listen to another man.

I gulped at the very thought of it. I didn't like the sound of it at all, being incarcerated in a little room with four big, snotty, intimidating, middle aged men who were all sulking with each other and me, who they would regard as a callow youth just out of college, telling them what to do. It did not sound like my idea of a good time at all but Miss Grieg needed help and I couldn't see any way of getting out of it without looking like an abject coward.

"Are you absolutely sure the will isn't here?" I asked in desperation.

"I'm quite sure, I posted it myself two days ago. The only other copy is in a bank vault in Cork and we can't get that until Monday morning at the earliest and that's of no use to us now."

My thoughts flew back to my professor of Medicine, Professor W.J.P.R. Soames. He had many wise word of advice to cover most eventualities that he often repeated to us students.

"Ladies and Gentlemen, the Art of Medicine is all about dealing with people and, on the whole, many people are difficult and odd. As a result, you are going to have many difficult and odd problems throughout your medical career to contend with. Sometimes there's only one way to deal with those problems and that is to take them on the chin. Just take them on the chin and get on with it. As Winston Churchill put it, 'When you're going through hell, keep going.'"

There was very much of the taking it on the chin and going through hell aspect about this problem. I sighed and agreed I would come back in an hour and meet the four men.

There were several expensive looking cars in the drive outside the Nursing Home when I returned an hour later. I was met by Matron who seemed relieved to see me.

"Oh, thank goodness you're back," she said. "The Forsythe brothers all arrived within minutes of each other shortly after you left. Not one of them acknowledged the other. I've put them in the sitting room with a pot of tea and some sandwiches and told them you'd be back shortly to explain everything to them. You could have cut the atmosphere in that room with a knife when I left. It'll be a lot worse now."

I liked the sound of that even less, especially the bit about the atmosphere. I felt I was being propelled into something that resembled a volcano about to erupt. For a brief second, I had an overwhelming urge to turn and run, jump into the Landover and drive off into the sunset.

Matron must have sensed my feelings. She gripped my arm tightly and escorted me up the corridor. I walked to the room like a condemned man. When I opened the door, it was worse than I expected. I immediately sensed a wall of hostility.

Four immensely tall men in dark suits and black overcoats were pacing around restlessly like tigers in a zoo, staring at anything other than at each other. They were waiting impatiently for me to arrive. As soon as I entered the room, they surrounded me like a pack of wolves.

"Well, Doctor," one of them said in an expensive public school accent, his voice full of impatience, "I understand that in the event of my father's final instructions being misplaced, you are in a position to tell us what his last wishes were." The man spoke with authority. He was obviously used to getting what he wanted.

I tried to swallow but my mouth was too dry. To my relief I discovered Miss Grieg had not abandoned me and had followed me into the room.

"Gentlemen," she said as I tried to find my voice, "as I explained to you earlier, Dr Griffin and myself were closely involved with the care and management of your father over the last several months. He gave us precise instructions about the disposal of his remains."

She went on to give these details to the men at length and finished by turning to me and saying, "Is that how you understood it, Dr Griffin?"

I would have agreed to almost anything.

"Yes indeed, Miss Grieg. Those were his very words. He said he wanted his remains brought straight from Slievegart to Cork funeral parlour and....."

My words were suddenly drowned out by Sadie charging into the room like a rampaging hippopotamus.

The Forsythe brothers all stepped back in unison and stared down at her with a look of disbelief. Sadie's sudden, uninvited appearance was an outrage to them at a time like this. They looked at her with such disdain, it was as though they thought she was going to paint a moustache on one of their Matisses or juggle with their priceless Ming vase.

Sadie was sublimely oblivious to their feelings as she made a beeline for the table and grabbed the remaining sandwiches they had left on the tray. She shoved them into her mouth two at a time and bolted them down with relish before becoming aware of the men's presence. Without batting an eyelid, she walked over to the biggest of them and tilting her head back looked up into his eyes, "Here you, big lad," she said pulling his arm to get his attention, "have you had your dinner yet?"

The man jerked back as if he had been slapped across his face. He didn't answer

"Hey you there, big lad, I'm talking to you. I said have you had your dinner yet?" Sadie repeated, pulling the man's sleeve even harder.

The man realised he would have to say something or she would go on pestering him. "Well no, not yet actually," he said.

"Well, guess what," Sadie said triumphantly, "I've had mine. I had it ages ago."

She went round each of the brothers in turn and asked them the same question about their dinner. Every time they said they hadn't eaten yet, she roared with jubilation and clapped her fat hands together. By the time she reached the last brother, I couldn't stop myself laughing. I had to leave the room in a hurry. To my surprise, Miss Grieg was right behind me. We met at the end of the corridor and laughed until the tears ran down our faces. It took a glass of water before I felt I could face the brothers again without chuckling. As we made our way back, Sadie came up the corridor looking very pleased with herself.

"Doctor, Doctor," she called when she saw me.

"What is it, Sadie?"

"Do you see them big men in that room. Not one of them has had his dinner yet and guess what."

"What Sadie?" I asked although I had an idea what the answer would be.

"I've had my dinner. And do you know something else, Doctor?"

"What Sadie?"

"They haven't had their tea either. And do you know what else?"

"What else Sadie?" I asked hoping she hadn't gone through the day's menu with them.

"I've had my tea already," and she slapped her thigh with delight. As far as she was concerned, she had got one over on the Forsythe brothers big as they were.

Miss Grieg and I composed ourselves and went back into the sitting room. The atmosphere had changed. It wasn't exactly friendly but the icy chill had gone. The brothers seemed somehow more relaxed. One was even offering another a cigarette.

Mr Forsythe was buried as he had wished. I don't know if the brothers ever became the best of friends but I do know one thing. Sadie had certainly helped to break the ice between them.

The Expert

There was a loud crack like the branch of a tree breaking.

"Oh no," I said to myself, "somebody has broken a leg."

I'd heard the same noise several years earlier when watching a Rugby match in College Park in Dublin. Once heard it's never forgotten.

I looked at the two footballers sprawled on the ground. One was a big man in his early thirties. I'd never seen him before. He was rolling round on the ground grasping one of his knees. He was obviously in pain. I knew the other player. He was a young man called Jerry who worked in the local petrol station. Jerry seemed remarkably well considering he was slightly built and had made a reckless flying tackle against an opponent who was much bigger and heavier than himself. He had rolled on to his stomach and was looking at the other man with a grin on his face as though enjoying seeing the other man in pain.

I was beginning to think I had made a mistake about the broken bone when I saw Jerry's face turn ashen as if a curtain of pain had been pulled down over it. He suddenly gripped the long grass and started to scream. I couldn't believe the change in him. He must have had a huge surge of endorphins (internal pain killers) for several seconds after he broke his leg. The effect had worn off and now the two big broken bone ends were rubbing together in an agonising friction. The shrieks took us all unawares.

Several men immediately ran over to help him. I saw to my annoyance that Walter McWalter was leading the pack. He was the Slievegart know-all who put himself in charge of every emergency on the football field. It wasn't going to make any medical assistance I might offer any easier. All the same, there was no doubt now which player had broken his leg.

I took Bonnie for a walk every Friday evening either to the harbour or to the local Gaelic football pitch. I would let her loose to sniff round and gambol with the other dogs while I watched the Slievegart team play on their hillside football pitch.

The pitch was actually a field where cows or sheep grazed but once or twice a week, the animals would be rounded up so the team could play football on it. That kept the grass short but there was a downside to it. The field was liberally dotted with enormous, wet cowpats. Players often slipped on them and sometimes hurt themselves as a result. The more experienced players used the cowpats to their advantage and shoved their opponents head first into them. Getting your head covered in stinking, sticky green cow dung is not much fun particularly when the nearest shower is three miles away, although it made the spectators laugh. Cows were chased off the pitch before a match and back on afterwards.

The field itself was three miles out of town and had been lent to the club by a farmer. It sloped down a small hill that slanted towards the sea. Playing downhill was a distinct advantage especially if there was an off shore wind. It added twenty or thirty yards to each kick.

Gaelic football and hurling were played there. I enjoyed watching them both particularly when there was an important championship match between Slievegart and one of the neighbouring parishes. That was when the games were fast and furious. Local parish rivalry was a big thing in Kerry and a matter of considerable pride which explained Jerry's foolhardy tackle

"You'll regret that madcap challenge for a day or two, my young lad," I thought to myself as I ran over to him.

Walter was the first to reach the two injured men. He immediately assumed control. I could see his ruddy face beneath his cloth cap flushed with excitement. This was his moment. He was so happy to be in charge of another medical emergency, he could hardly contain himself.

"Right, right, right lads, we'll all need to calm ourselves down." He was so excited, he could hardly speak. "We've a sprain here at the very least and maybe a head injury as well."

Once he had got over his initial excitement and settled himself, Walter spoke with the confidence and authority of a senior consultant. On the two or three occasions I had seen him in action, his self-belief and self-assurance on medical matters took my breath away. He had no medical training whatsoever. He hadn't even done a course in first aid. Dr O'Flathertie disliked him intensely, probably because he was every bit as cocky as himself. He had very definite views about Walter MacWalter.

"That half wit MacWalter is a danger to society with that horse brand of medicine of his. He should be locked up every time there's a football match," he'd said when I told him I'd seen Walter in charge the previous evening. "If he had any brains he'd be dangerous. He thinks he's some sort of an honorary doctor because he's friends with that Doctor Mussen who's nearly as daft as he is. The sum total of MacWalter's experience is de-horning a few cattle and getting in the vet's way at the delivery of his neighbour's cows. He's an expert alright, an expert in self promotion."

I decided never to mention Walter to him again.

A small group of men had gathered round Jerry and the other man. That pleased Walter. He was where he wanted to be right in the middle of things, the centre of attention and the man in charge.

"Now lads, we have a situation here where we have two injured parties. We have to do what Dr Mussen calls triaging, In other words we have to deal with the man that has the worst injuries first and then the next and so on. Walter was warming up to a full-blown lecture. All that was missing was a podium. He seemed oblivious of Jerry who was screaming in agony. He barely glanced at him.

"By my reckoning, young Jerry O'Callaghan is the least injured party. Don't be distracted by his lamentable screams. That's what Dr Mussen calls part of the catastrophic syndrome, a sort of attention seeking. Now that big lad over there from Ballymaher," and Walter turned towards the big man who had

195

been hugging his knee a few seconds earlier, only to find that he had been helped to his feet and was hobbling toward the side line.

Walter was completely unfazed by his glaring error as he did an about turn and continued, "that lad is the sort of lad who will get to his own two feet as quick as a flash and, there you are. You've seen it in front of your own very eyes in the way I have just described."

None of the men seemed to have noticed Walter's gaffe. He had been going to football matches in the local parish for years and had built his reputation up. He was seen as a man who knew his medicine.

"Right, right now, calm yourself down a bit," he said as he switched his attention to the only casualty left – Jerry. "You're not that bad. There's no need for you to be screaming like a banshee." He knelt down beside him and tried to take hold of his wrist to check his pulse. Jerry screamed and thrashed his arms about in pain. Walter tut-tutted at the noise Jerry was making.

"Come on there, lad," he said, "keep the volume down a bit. The Ballymaher men will think the Slievegart footballers are a bunch of girls.

I had placed myself behind and to the side of Walter. I wanted to make sure he didn't do anything too foolish.

"Right men," he said, "his blood pressure is alright," Walter said.

"How can he know that by just looking at him," I wondered.

"Despite that I think by his pallor he's going into delayed shock. So we'll need to get the boots off and elevate the legs. Dr Mussen says that's the first priority in treating shock."

I groaned in exasperation at the crass stupidity of the man. It meant I would have to intervene and I knew how he would take that. How could anyone, even half sensible propose taking the boots off a man who had just broken his leg without giving him an anaesthetic and then to talk about lifting the leg in the air! Walter was reaching out to undo the laces when I called out.

"Hold on please. Hold on a minute. We'll not remove his boots just yet. Jerry's broken his leg and needs an ambulance."

Walter spun round. He was obviously cross at having his authority challenged.

"And who do you think you are, if you don't mind me asking?" he said raising his eyebrows in disapproval.

"I'm Dr Griffin."

"Dr Griffin," Walter spat the words out.

"Yes, Dr Griffin, I work for Dr Roberts. We'll need to get an ambulance."

"If you don't mind, young man, I have dealt with situations like this before and I'm quite aware of what is needed." Walter was not going to hand over to anyone without a fight.

I sighed. This was the sort of nonsense I couldn't be bothered with. I had a delicate line to tread to make sure that no harm came to Jerry and pussy footing round Walter's enormous ego. After all, I was not a local man and any slight to Walter could be construed as an insult to the people of Slievegart. I felt like shrugging my shoulders and going home.

I was about to ask someone to go down and phone for an ambulance when Walter turned to a man standing near him and said, "Francey, would you mind going down to Muldoon's lounge bar on your bicycle like a good man and putting a call through for an ambulance."

I had to admit Walter was a smooth operator as he did another perfect about turn. Francey nodded his head in deference to Walter's superior knowledge and ran off to look for his bike.

"We'll maybe leave his boots on, lads, for a minute while I check on Jerry's cardiac status. Dr Mussen says the first priority always has to be the coronary cardiac heart."

I was impressed by his use of medical words even if they meant nothing. "We might well have to take them boots off yet to stop swelling occurring in the peripheries. A swollen foot in a boot can be a dangerous conundrum and lead on to gangrene. That's what Dr Mussens says," Walter stated staring directly at me.

Jerry was still shouting at the top of his voice and thrashing about. There was little that could be done to ease the pain until the ambulance arrived. The weather had turned much cooler and a few drops of rain had started to fall out of a dark, forbidding sky. It looked like we were in for a drenching. I was going to suggest putting a folded jacket under Jerry's head and covered him with a blanket but decided to wait a minute until Walter had finished his examination. It would keep the peace at the price of a little discomfort.

I don't know what Walter was hoping to find with the examination he was carrying out. He was pressing lightly on the protesting patient's chest and nodding his head knowingly at the same time as though he was thinking to himself, 'Ah, just as I suspected.'

I wondered if he had any idea of what he was doing himself.

"Ah, as I thought," he said, "contusion and more contusions, maybe even internal contusions. That will make the shock worse."

I was flabbergasted by the man's capacity to believe his own nonsense. A contusion is simply another word for a bruise. How could he know there were bruises let alone internal ones unless he lifted Jerry's shirt up to look. Still it impressed the onlookers. They nodded their heads in agreement. Walter pulled his black briar pipe from his pocket and shoved it into his mouth as he sat and contemplated Jerry. What would his next move be, I wondered. I decided to risk proposing the pillow and blanket. Jerry was beginning to look very uncomfortable. As soon as I spoke, Walter looked at me coldly. He didn't like my suggestion about the blanket although he did take off his own jacket and put it under Jerry's head.

"Dr Mussen says in all cases of shock you cannot and I repeat cannot, be too careful. He has often told me that many doctors, particularly G.P.s are not aware of how to treat shock. They attempt to warm the patient up and that makes the shock worse and sometimes brings on delayed shock."

I nodded my head as if I agreed with him as I thought 'what a load of cods wallop.'

"Do you know Dr Mussen, young man?" he asked looking directly at me.

"I'm afraid I don't," I told him.

"Dr Mussen is a very great doctor, a very great doctor indeed. I might say one of the best doctors in Ireland if not in the entire British Isles as a whole. He was a great sportsman in his day and played rugby for Munster. Now there's a man who knows a thing or two about sports injuries. He's seen them all in fifty years of practice and dealt with them all too. Dr Mussen has taught me a great deal of what he knows."

Walter was looking at me as he spoke but he was actually addressing the small crowd standing around impressing them with his learning and making them aware of his impeccable qualifications. I could see that they were impressed.

"Now I know, young man, you are working with Dr Roberts. I hear he's a good doctor but he's not my doctor, no indeed. Dr Mussen's my doctor, he always has been and always will be. He's a very knowledgeable man and a specialist especially where the treatment of shock is concerned.

I'd had about all I could take of his Dr Mussen and Dr Mussen's unparalleled knowledge particularly in the management of shock. Jerry was starting to shiver despite the fact he was still flailing about. That meant he was getting cold. It was time to put a blanket or a jacket over him. I took my coat off and, stepping around Walter, spread it over Jerry's chest.

"What do you think you're doing?" Walter snapped.

"I'm covering Jerry up. He's freezing and it's starting to rain and he'll get even colder." I didn't want to hear any more of his nonsense about shock.

"Dr Mussen says that a perspiring sportsman does not need to be covered up no matter what the weather. It stimulates the phagocytes and causes adhesion of the red and white corpuscles which aggravate the shock," Walter was really surpassing himself. Either Dr Mussen was the most brainless doctor in

Ireland if he really had said all that twaddle or Walter was seriously deluded. Either way that coat was staying on. Walter tried to pull it off.

"Please leave the coat alone," I said as I leaned forward and firmly pulled it back over Jerry's chest. I held it there until Walter gave up trying to remove it. If it hadn't been so serious, it would have been laughable, two grown men arguing about the position of a coat. When Walter realised I wasn't going to give in, he relit his pipe and sat back on his haunches smoking it.

It started to rain heavily. "Where is that ambulance?" I wondered. It was a good forty five minutes since Francey had set off on his bike. It wasn't only that I was concerned about Jerry, I wanted to get away from Walter and his silly ego games.

He continued to huff while I looked at Jerry's leg. I could see the indentation where the tibia bone had snapped just above the ankle. It would take a few months for that to heal properly I was thinking when Walter took the pipe from his mouth and spoke.

"And how long have you been qualified, Dr Griffin?"

I wondered what he was up to asking me that when five minutes earlier he had been in a fit of the sulks.

"About fifteen months," I answered carefully.

"Fifteen months," Walter smiled indulgently, "fifteen months isn't a long time is it?" He damped down his pipe and blew out a stream of rank blue smoke. "It's hard to beat a bit of experience is what I always say, especially when it comes to the treatment of shock. Dr Mussen, now there's a man who knows everything there is to know about shock. He's been dealing with sports injuries and shock for fifty years now. He knows what's he's on about. No, as far as I'm concerned you can have your book learning. Give me the man with experience every time."

I had heard that sort of nonsense before. A short time in practice had taught me there are an awful lot of people who are experts with other people's injuries or illnesses but when it's themselves in trouble, they tend to rush to the nearest doctor. With other people's ailments, they are confident, knowledgeable and full of helpful advice. Another phenomenon I noticed was that their advice is often regarded as more valuable than the doctor's, like now. Walter, for instance, was obviously an accepted sage on the management of shock and the onlookers listened to everything he said, almost with reverence.

It grew colder and colder. I slapped my arms to try and keep warm. We stood huddled round Jerry sheltering him as the rain poured down in torrents. He had stopped thrashing around and seemed in less pain as long as he remained perfectly still.

"What about my leg, Doctor?" he managed to gasp. "Is it broken?"

"Yes, it's broken, Jerry," I replied, "it's......"

"It's more of a fracture, Jerry," Walter cut in. His brow was wrinkled as if he had given it much thought.

"Is it fractured as well, Doctor," Jerry asked in alarm.

It was a difficult question to answer without looking as if I was hedging in the face of Walter's knowledge. The problem was that a broken bone and a fractured bone are one and the same thing. Many non medical people think they refer to two different conditions but they don't. Some see a broken bone as more serious while others think a fractured bone is worse. I didn't want to get into an argument with Walter about the difference especially as the rain was now lashing down.

"Whether it's broken or fractured, Jerry, the treatment will be much the same," I told him.

Walter looked round at the onlookers, his eyes wide open in disbelief that I could say something so patently stupid. He shrugged his shoulders as if to say, "There, do you see now what I mean. It's hopeless. He's just a know nothing." Jerry was the only one who seemed to have any confidence in me, Maybe it was because I always chatted to him when I bought petrol or maybe it was because I had stopped Walter removing his boots.

"What do you think they'll do with my leg?" he asked.

"You'll be seen by a surgeon in Tralee who'll decide when he's studied the X-ray whether to put you in plaster or insert a pin into the two pieces of bone to hold them together."

I didn't like to tell him that what would happen to him would depend a lot on the experience of the surgeon who treated him.

Walter gave a sarcastic laugh. "There'll be no plaster of Paris job there, young man, you take my word for it. Dr Mussen says you might as well put putty on a fractured leg as that plaster of Paris, a complete waste of time that plaster. That's what he says."

I was cold, tired and hungry and I was sure Jerry was as well. Walter's relentless carping was starting to get to me. I could feel the anger flooding through me like a raging fire at his constant nit picking. I felt like picking up the biggest cowpat I could find and rubbing it in his face. Instead, I clenched my teeth and said nothing.

The wind was now howling in gusts up the hill side. It was like a late autumn gale. A woman brought over a blanket and an umbrella and we were able to protect Jerry from the worst of the weather. I spread the blanket over him despite Walter's muttering about shock and Dr Mussen.

An hour and a half after Francey had gone to call the ambulance, it arrived. Walter was bedraggled and as cold as the rest of us as we watched Jerry being put in the back of the ambulance. I had to give it to him though. He had stayed at his post without deserting the patient which was more than a lot of the other spectators had done. As the ambulance drove off, he had the last word.

"If he survives the shock," he said to his four remaining cronies, speaking loudly for my benefit, "It'll be a pin job for young O'Callaghan in the morning."

Walter was right. Jerry did get a pin in his leg. The reason might have been because the surgeon on duty was a young man with a lot of orthopaedic training. If one of the older surgeons had seen him, he'd have slapped him straight away into plaster. Walter's standing in the community as a medical man soared. After all, wasn't he the man who had predicted a pin for Jerry when young Dr Griffin was rabbiting on about a plaster cast and didn't he explain the treatment of shock to him as well?

Despite my promise never to mention Walter to Dr O'Flathertie again, I had to let off steam to somebody when I met him a day or two later. He was sympathetic and always referred to Walter after that as, 'the man who knows too many things.'

Home

"James, are you coming home or not? You promised to do a two month's locum for me in November."

It was my father phoning to make sure I hadn't forgotten him

"No, I'm not. I've got a job working on a cruise ship in the Mediterranean for six months and I'm starting next week."

There was a noise like a mini explosion on the other end of the phone. "What are you talking about. You promised you'd help your mother and me out. What are we going to do now?" He sounded completely exasperated.

"I'm only joking," I said, "I'll be home on Thursday when Dr Roberts gets back."

"I suppose that's your flying snake humour again," he said through gritted teeth.

"Monty Python, father," I said patiently, "Monty Python." It was a conversation that was repeated frequently. "And yes, I'm having a great time and how are you and everyone else at home?"

"Thursday then," he snapped. "You're sure you'll be there?"

"I'm sure."

"Thursday it is then," and he put the phone down. My father wasn't the chatty type.

Two days later, Dr Roberts returned from his holiday looking sun burnt and ten years younger. He was more buoyant than ever. He hooted as he turned into the drive, I went and opened the front door for them.

Bonnie bounded out and nearly knocked him down in her joy at seeing him as she jumped up and down. Her months of loyalty to me had evaporated in a matter of seconds. Dr Roberts was nearly as happy to see her as she was to see him. When he got Bonnie settled, he handed me a daintily wrapped parcel and said, "Here you are, James. That's a little thank you for all the work you've done for me."

At first I thought it was an expensive French aftershave although it was an odd shape. Then I caught a pungent whiff that was definitely not aftershave.

"Go on, James, open it," he urged me.

I opened it cautiously to find it contained a sausage, an enormous, shrivelled sausage. I didn't know what to say as I stood looking at it.

"Well. Do you like it?"

I didn't know what it was so I it was hard to say whether I liked it or not. I knew by the way they were both looking at me, they expected some kind of response.

"Oh, yes, I really like it. It's great" I said with as much enthusiasm as I could muster. I was going to add it was what I had always wanted but I thought that could be going a bit too far.

"It's Andouille," he said, obviously pleased with himself for producing such a rarity.

"Andouille?" I repeated.

"Yes, Andouille. It's a specialty of Lower Normandy. It's a type of sheep tripe."

"Sheep tripe?"

"Yes James. You know what tripe is, sheep's intestines boiled in a special way. Well this is the best sheep tripe in the world with spices added. The French won the prize for being the world's best tripe makers in a little town in Normandy called Vire in 1966 and that's where I bought your tripe. It's the best I've ever tasted. I love it. I must have eaten a ton of it when I was in France. It goes down a treat with a drop of Calvados brandy."

"I must try that some time," thinking as I spoke that one of my friends was getting married in a few weeks time and this might be just the ticket for a wedding present with a difference.

"Well how did you get on while I was away?" he asked as we settled down in the lounge.

I told him about Dr O'Flathertie's idea of a cure for Charlie O'Shea and he laughed uproariously.

"Dr O'Flathertie, well now, he's his own man. He has the quarest of treatments at times that have never been written up in any of the medical textbooks but they seem to work a treat, nevertheless".

When he heard about Anton Mors' death and the subsequent fiasco followed by Kitty's death three weeks later, the smile left his face and he sat silently for a long time. When he eventually spoke, he wiped a tear from his eye.

"Ah, James, James," he said with great feeling. "Anton Mor O'Sullivan, Anton Mor, I am saddened to hear he has died. He was a man if ever I met one, a man among men. He would have been King of all Ireland if he had been born at the right time and his wife, Kitty dead too. She was a beautiful woman. I never met a couple like them, striking in every way.

We had many a great yarn together over the years, Ypres, the Somme, Passchendale. He was at them all and knew everything about them. He had a degree of compassion and humility I never saw before in any man. He was a shining example to us all." He sat staring into the distance, completely lost in thought.

I was touched by the doctor's depth of feeling for his patients. I could see why they all loved him.

However, life has to go on. I had to go home the following morning to help my father out whatever the sadness I felt at leaving.

It was with a heavy heart I took the train back to Dublin the following morning and caught a connection to Belfast. I felt I was leaving behind a rare and special time in my life that could never be repeated. I knew I had been privileged to have the chance to work in such a beautiful place with such lovely people. As the poet, Tomas O'Cronin from the Great Blasket Island which is off the coast of Kerry, once said, "You will never see our likes again."

My father met me at the station. He looked exhausted and in need of a holiday. No wonder he hadn't been chatty on the phone.

As we drove over the hills of the Black Mountains that overlooked Belfast I was still feeling gloomy at leaving behind the sweeping Kerry Mountains and the crashing seas.

I was surprised to see how rich and fertile the land of my birth was. My memories of County Antrim were hazy. It was over thirteen years since I had left, what with going to school and University and, apart from the occasional day or two over Christmas and the odd visit, I had few memories of the countryside. As we drove into the village of Clonavon an unexpected nostalgia enveloped me as I saw many of the places where I had played as a boy, the river where I had fished with my friends and the trees we had climbed together.

My mother was delighted to see me and had a celebratory meal laid on. I tried to get the two of them to sample a piece of Dr Robert's Andouille.

"Thank you, James, maybe some other time," my mother said politely while my father told me bluntly to keep it for myself. It looked like the Andouille was going to finish up as a wedding present after all.

I went for a walk around the village that evening. It had hardly changed since I had moved away. I was surprised at how peaceful it was and how beautiful the countryside around was. I suppose I had taken it all for granted when I was a young lad. I certainly hadn't appreciated the colours and the simple beauty of the area.

The village was one long street that reached over the brow of a small hill. It used to be known as The Village of the Long Street. It was said that one of the followers of St Patrick had founded a Church in the village in the fifth century beside the Clonavon River and it is said the Church that stands there today, St Andrews, Church of Ireland, was built on that site.

Most of the houses along the street were single storey and built of grey granite. The only businesses of any note was the shop, the pharmacy and a pub although the pub always seemed to be closed. As a boy, I watched men dressed in dark clothes and riding black bicycles coming occasionally to the pub door.

They would put their bikes against the door and rap on it. The door would open just wide enough to admit them but we never saw who opened it.

A man called Gilbert McSweeney ran the only shop in the street. He was a big, jolly man with a bushy beard. He always wore a collar and tie and a green shop coat. Everyone liked him. He was not a man to curse or say a bad word about anybody. His shop sold everything from pork chops and brandy balls, to Tilley lamps and diesel engines. If he didn't have what you wanted, he would get it for you by the end of the week.

The shop was the kind that children love. It looked small from the front but the further you went into it, the more nooks and crannies you would find where you could discover all sorts of things hidden away. In the summer, Gilbert put up a red and white striped awning with flowers and gardening tools beneath it.

Just a couple of doors up from him was the chemist shop run by a man called Ballantine. I used to watch him through the big glass windows of his shop making up pungent looking medicines from enormous glass bottles with strange names written on them. He always sang as he mixed them. He had a deep baritone voice and you could hear him singing from the end of the street.

The village was very quiet that night. There was hardly any traffic and a group of boys were playing football in the middle of the road just as I used to when I was their age, always keeping an eye open for Sergeant Milligan on his bicycle doing his rounds. I walked for a long time, thinking of the past and, only then, appreciating what a happy, carefree childhood I had experienced in such peaceful surroundings.

I passed over the three arched bridge that spanned the Clonavon river and looked down to see if there were any trout in the water. I had often spent the day there with friends, wading barefoot up and down in the water with our nets and jam jars looking for sticklebacks. We didn't go home until our stomachs were aching with hunger and our feet blue with cold.

I left the village and started to climb the road that took me to the top of the Hill of Crewe, the highest point, at 629 feet.

in the district. The Kings of Ulster were said to have been crowned there. From the summit, I could see an enormous area of the countryside spread out in front of me. The hill sloped down to the distant shores of Lough Neagh and to the north, I glimpsed the blue hills of the Sperrin Mountains. To the south, the mountains of Mourne swept down to the Irish Sea. The Black Mountains were to the east and when I looked westward, there was a rich tapestry of green and yellow and golden fields. Could there have been anywhere better for the Kings of Ulster to be crowned.

The famous Country and Western singer, Johnny Cash, once visited Ireland and wrote a song afterwards called "Forty Shades of Green." As I looked down the valley that evening, I thought there were many more shades of green than forty. I suppose Johnny figured that eighty seven shades didn't sound quite as catchy as forty.

Our house was a large red brick one. It had been built on a hill just outside the village and was surrounded by an expanse of green fields. The house had a long avenue up the steep hill which tested the lungs of anyone visiting us on foot. There was a front garden with two enormous cherry trees and numerous bushes and flower beds.

The cherry trees blossomed in May with an explosion of palest pink. Later, when the winds blew, the blossom drifted down like snow flakes and formed a thick carpet on the ground. My sisters used to gather it in handfuls and throw it over each other like confetti. It was a perfect place to play games like hide and seek.

The back garden was a football pitch bordered by a line of beech and ash trees which I climbed many times as a boy. I could still see the remnants of the tree house my father had built us, now reduced to a few haphazard planks. The back garden had often echoed to the sounds of children shrieking and squealing with excitement as we played football or rode our bikes over home made ramps with our friends.

The surgery was a converted garage that stood beside the house. It contained two consulting rooms and a small waiting room that seated eight people and a tiny office for the part-time receptionist. If more than eight people came into the waiting room, they had to stand, either there or on the steps outside. As the knees of the people sitting in the waiting room almost touched each other, they didn't have much space for standing.

The district nurse was called Bella and the part time receptionist was Ida. At eleven o'clock each morning, my mother invited them into our kitchen for a cup of tea and some biscuits. We children had to stay outside then and, on no account were we allowed to ask for a biscuit.

Ida had been working for my father for fourteen years when I went there as a locum. She was a small, plump woman with short, permed hair. She would have been about fifty then. She always wore tweed clothes and sensible shoes and, whenever she went out, she wore a hat that looked like the funnel of a ship.

She spoke slowly, always pronouncing every word very carefully. When I first met her, I thought she was boring and one of the most humourless people I had ever met but, when I got to know her, I realised I couldn't have been more wrong.

Before she went to work for my father, she had been a librarian and had given up her job to look after her husband who was dying of cancer. Ida wasn't one of my father's patients but he got to hear that she was suffering from depression after the death of her husband. My father was always an impulsive man and he immediately got into his car and went round to her house. When she answered the door, he didn't give her a chance to say a word.

"Ida," he said, "I need you to come and help me in the surgery as a part time secretary."

She looked at him with surprise, "But I know nothing about being a medical secretary," she protested, "I'm a librarian."

"You'll have great organising and filing skills then, don't you? Can you type?"

"No, I'm sorry, I can't."

"Don't worry about that. You'll soon pick it up. I'll get Mrs Nelson to give you a couple of lessons, she used to teach typing at the Tech. Can you start on Monday?"

"Monday? Isn't that a bit soon?" Ida was obviously flustered

"Well Tuesday then. I'll see you at nine o'clock. We'll sort out the salary later."

My mother had been working as his secretary although she also acted as a doctor as well. She wasn't a bit pleased that my father had appointed somebody else without discussing it with her.

"You'll have no need to answer the phone or front door any more or hand out prescriptions Joan," he told her obviously pleased with himself. Despite his explanation, my mother felt she had been ousted from her role. Ida hadn't been in the surgery for more than an hour before my mother realised what an asset she was and what a burden had been taken off her shoulders.

Ida took to the job like a duck to water. She knew everything and everyone in Clonavon, knew where they lived and who was married to who, the blood relationships between different families and everything that was happening in the countryside around Clonavon.

When I started working as a locum, I found her encyclopedic knowledge invaluable especially for the first few months until I started to recognise and remember some of the families and characters.

I started work the following Monday. I was glad I had a couple of days to familiarise myself with the surgery and to reacquaint myself with the people and the countryside. I didn't want another experience of being plunged in at the deep end like I had in County Kerry.

It was a strange feeling as I settled in. It was almost as if I had never been away from Clonavon. I felt as though I had been travelling towards this point, this place – where I was born – all my life.